OCCUPIED GUERNSEY
1943 - 1945

Occupied Guernsey
1943-1945
'The Final Record'

by Herbert Winterflood

The Guernsey Press and Star

Printed & Bound in Great Britain by MPG Books Ltd, Bodmin, Cornwall

Produced by MSP Channel Islands, a division of The Guernsey Press
& Star, Braye Road, Vale, Guernsey, GY1 3BW. 2005©

© The Guernsey Press Company Limited.
ISBN 0-9539116-6-7

Preface

IN the first edition of "Occupied Guernsey", the unique story of the German occupation of Guernsey covering the period from July 1940 to December 1942 was told through extracts from the *Guernsey Evening Press* cuttings.

It was a time when the German military was establishing itself throughout the Channel Islands, and when the civilian populations were learning to cope with shortages of food, medical supplies and materials of all kinds.

Improvisation was the keynote of the time, and many islanders received congratulations on developing inventions, which helped to preserve in some degree a reasonable standard of living.

In Guernsey, half the population of some 40,000 souls evacuated to the United Kingdom. Sark kept all its 400 islanders, but in Alderney the entire population, with the exception of a handful of civilians, left their homes for the mainland. A proportion of Jersey residents decided to evacuate, and of course all the islands were left wide open to the German Forces as they advanced rapidly through France.

The troops were able to enter all the islands in the group without a shot being fired as they had been declared open towns without defensive systems in place.

In this second book, I have followed the same method of working as I did in the first edition – reading through the newspapers of the day and extracting items which, in my view, illustrated the difficulties to be encountered during the five long years of occupation.

It should be explained that both the *Guernsey Evening Press* and the *Guernsey Star* newspapers were subject to strict censorship, so many of the military events of those times are not recorded. These are to be found in other publications, for example details of British commando raids on Sark and Guernsey, and also in newspaper articles contributed both by myself and others.

However, this is the first time that anybody has read through the wartime newspapers of the 1940-1945 conflict and committed extracts to print.

This book of press cuttings takes the reader through the more difficult years of the occupation when very serious shortages were being experienced.

With the advancement of Allied troops through Normandy after D-Day on 6 June 1944, the Channel Islands became under siege as shipping from St. Malo could not use that port to bring much-needed supplies to Guernsey, Jersey and Sark.

It was indeed the arrival of the Vega at Christmas 1944 that saved the day for islanders. She brought Red Cross parcels, flour and medical supplies on this and following visits. Such supplies enabled islanders to avoid complete starvation and to enable them to greet British forces with great enthusiasm on 9 May 1945 when church bells rang out the joyous message of freedom.

It was the editor of the *Guernsey Press*, Richard Digard, who invited me to scan the occupation newspapers and snatch items of interest from their yellowing pages.

The first edition has sold extremely well, although copies can still be obtained. In the first preface, it was promised that if the first book sold well, consideration would be given to a second and final edition concluding the five years of German domination.

Well, we have kept our promise and here is that second edition completing the record of the time when the Channel Islands had no connections with Britain for five long years.

Herbert Winterflood

Another year of war

THE Comment column of the *Guernsey Evening Press* on 4 January 1943 recorded the fact that, because of the curfew imposed by the occupying forces, jollification both at Christmas and New Year had to take place in island homes.

The writer thought that this was a good thing, as prior to the war we were tending too much towards synthetic entertainments such as dances.

'Although these were good in a way, they never captured the true spirit of the day. Are not house parties far more satisfying to young and old than outside entertainment?' queried the writer.

I don't know what he would make of the outside entertainment offered for young and old during the festive season now.

The scribe went on to suggest that in some countries, New Year's Day was a time for informal visiting but suggested that Guernsey people were too formal and conservative to foster the custom of unheralded visiting.

However, he was delighted to report that some people did roam the island during the 1943 festivities, taking food with them to ensure a good welcome.

There appears to have been some mixed storing of potatoes with paraffin, as a reader signing himself 'Hungry' complained that in the last ration of potatoes, half of the spuds were uneatable because of a strong taste of paraffin. The writer emphasised that this was not an isolated case.

Last year, I recorded that the former Lyric Cinema had been converted into a theatre with good results. In January 1943, it was reported that the theatre was celebrating its birthday with a production by the Amherstian Players entitled 'While Parents Sleep'.

There was a big demand for seats, evidently by parents who really wanted to discover what the young ones were doing while they slept.

Meanwhile, the Regal Players were rehearsing for the production, 'Ghost Train'.

For those people who were permitted to burn petrol, the price from 4 January would be 4s 10d per gallon. During the festive holiday period, there were two thefts of tobacco and cigarettes from Bucktrout's. Some 20,000 cigarettes were stolen and a heavy weight of tobacco. The police issued a description of the cigarette packets in the hope of finding the culprits if they risked selling the smokes. Although traffic was fairly light on the roads, it was necessary always to keep a sharp lookout. It was reported that a road sweeper had been knocked over by a lorry at L'Aumone crossroads, suffering severe head injuries.

A report stated that heavy luggage, which had not accompanied people deported from the island in 1942, would now have arrived at camps where they were detained. Before leaving the island, efforts had been made to ensure that each unit of baggage was secure through binding with rope.

At this stage in the Occupation, the *Press* carried large numbers of small advertisements from people wishing to buy or exchange, such as vinegar for cigarettes or a gross of pre-war matches for tobacco.

Both the local police and the German police had been very active and successful in putting a gang of men under lock and key.

They alleged that such men were responsible for a series of raids on food stores.

However, they wanted the gang's leader and Acting Inspector Albert Lamy issued a picture of the man, who was said to be French and without an identity card.

He was described as 'a cat burglar of the most daring type'. Readers were asked to help catch the thief by reporting any sighting. He was thought to be in the St Peter Port area. If he continued with his stealing, it was feared that the island's food supplies would be seriously depleted.

In times of great difficulty, the authorities of any country are never fearful of issuing stern laws.

During the Occupation, Guernsey was no exception. Legislation was approved by the Royal Court to combat soaring prices. A maximum price was issued for various articles and there would be a penalty for anybody exceeding such amounts. The order applied to traders, auctioneers, restaurant owners, etc and people advertising in the newspapers would be obliged to put their proper names with each advert. The German authorities had readily agreed to the restrictions.

There were some items that would be exempt from the order.

Auctioneers were warned that if an item increased above the maximum price listed and was paid by the bidder, both the auctioneer and the bidder would be liable for prosecution. Traders were told that items exposed for sale had to bear the asking price in clear figures.

I just wonder how the black market racket responded to such control?

Not much to buy, but at least the price was fair

AS SUPPLIES became less available to the general public, every effort was being made to ensure that people were not paying over the odds.

For instance, in early February 1943, a grower from the north of the island was summoned for overcharging for dried beans and onions.

He pleaded not guilty, suggesting that the persons in question had refused to take change. However, the case against him was proved and he was fined £2.

The court heard that the grower had already been before the magistrate on a similar summons.

The text of a letter from an airman who had been shot down over Holland was reproduced in the *Evening Press* on 1 February 1943. It was received by Mr and Mrs James Bichard, of the Green Lanes and was from their son, Pilot Officer Herbert Bichard. The letter revealed that he had joined the RAF in 1940 and on 6 December 1942, his aircraft was shot down by German fighters. Two of his crew were wounded and another killed. He revealed that he was in a POW camp mainly for officers and there were Guernsey chaps with him. While such letters were arriving in Guernsey, there were no Red Cross messages leaving the island. Owing to the non-arrival of the necessary forms from Paris, the sending of monthly messages was suspended until further notice.

Nobody was going to suffer from writer's cramp.

The States Dairy was in urgent need of rubber boots for the staff. All sizes were required for both sexes and a good price would be offered.

Mr W. D. M. Lovell, the clothing controller, revealed to the *Evening Press* that carefully laid plans were in place, which should ease the problem for all men, women and children in respect of woollen underclothes.

Over 2,000 pairs of workmen's trousers had been made from

material obtained in France. Also a mixed bag of second-hand clothing had been collected locally and had been sorted and priced. In addition, men's pullovers and socks had been made in fairly large quantities. People were being encouraged to rip up old jumpers and use the wool to make new ones. Bramble leaves, presumably for making 'tea', were on sale from Mr A. W. Hughes at 8d per lb. The Germans seemed to have plenty of sympathy for those who wished to enjoy boxing tournaments. On 15 February, they agreed to extend the curfew hour to 11pm so that boxing could go ahead at the Regal Cinema.

It was ormering time and people who ventured onto permitted beaches either enjoyed a feast or sold the shellfish at 6s per dozen. This worked out at 2s for two on a plate but the *Evening Press* reckoned that consumers voted the charge very worthwhile. One ormer gathering exploit ended in death. A small party of men from Torteval, an inquest was told, ignored mine warning signs. One youth of 17 trod on a mine and was killed, while another member of the group was badly injured.

The coroner blamed the men for not taking notice of the warning boards.

The *Evening Press* announced that traffic control had resumed at important road junctions. Those involved wore white armbands.

I can't imagine that they were very busy.

A bartering restriction was introduced by the States in respect of firewood. None could be bartered for other goods and no such product could be advertised either for barter or sale.

People breaking the order, necessary to conserve stocks of such wood, could be fined up to £100 or jailed for up to six months.

Islanders were being encouraged to grow more potatoes.

The States had a fine supply of seed potatoes. Prices to growers were to be guaranteed and therefore spuds would be the most profitable crop to produce.

The German Commandant issued an order in respect of the private letting of premises to workers employed by the

Organisation Todt or other German organisations. All such arrangements were made by the authority in charge. Any person found helping foreign workers to find lodgings privately or offering such accommodation could be fined or imprisoned for up to six weeks.

Tortevalites jailed for attempt to hog a pig

SOME islanders were up to various tricks, either to make more money or to get additional food, as the newspapers of February 1943 revealed.

Three men and a woman from Torteval were before the Magistrate over a pig killing fraud. They conspired to obtain possession of half a pig, thus defrauding the Essential Commodities Committee. Further, they attempted to obtain pork by making a statement, knowing that it was false.

The court was told that the police had received a telephone call to the effect that a pig had been killed and half the body, which had hung in a greenhouse, had been stolen.

One of the defendants said he had later broken into the greenhouse and taken the carcass to a friend's shed. The idea was to make it appear that a burglary had taken place. Short prison sentences and fines were imposed on the defendants.

A farmer from the north was summoned for supplying sugar without authority and selling sugar above the maximum price laid down. He was fined £30.

Things were no better in Jersey – a farmer there was fined £20 for watering down his milk.

Another reported that he had lost a 10-month-old heifer from his stable while he was enjoying his tea.

Mr A. J. Laine, the chairman of the Prices Determination Committee, issued a warning to public house managers and catering establishments about the need to display a list of maximum prices for their products. This was one way of keeping inflation down.

Civil Transport responded to a reader's letter to run evening bus services to country parishes. People were warned that if certain routes were not patronised, they would be withdrawn without notice. The only tickets available would be returns.

The States warned gas users that, if they used more than their ration, they faced the risk of the supply being cut off without warning. It was agreed that the majority of islanders were sticking to the amount of gas laid down but others were burning it to excess.

The Germans issued a lengthy order aimed at the protection of the Occupying Authority. Newspapers should not discredit the German Reich; pamphlets should not be issued without military permission and no outdoor photographs should be taken.

'They conspired to obtain possession of half a pig, thus defrauding the Essential Commodities Committee'

These were just a few of the restrictions in the order. Attacks on members of the German Armed Forces could be punishable by death. Two pages of the *Evening Press* were taken up by this order, which was printed both in German and English.

The Germans seemed very keen to acquire horses. They ordered that anybody thinking of selling such a creature born before 1 January 1940 should first offer it to the German Commandant. If he was not interested, then it could be sold to a civilian. If a horse was sold without first contacting the Commandant, then the sale would be classed as illegal. A fine or imprisonment or both could follow. The horse could not object to working for the enemy.

A man who appeared before the Magistrate's Court for not sending his children to school regularly said that the problem developed because they had no serviceable shoes. The defendant was given a month to find suitable footwear for his daughters.

Chilblains were again in the news, one woman stating that she had cured members of her family of the complaint by applying a mixture of zinc and castor oil ointment to the affected parts.

A chemist then came forth with the information that both ill-fitting shoes and gloves caused chilblains. A fatal thing to do was to warm hands by a fire or hot pipes before venturing out into the cold air.

Playboy, the theatre critic for the *Guernsey Press*, came down a bit heavily on Peter Campbell's production 'A Little Bit of Fluff,' staged by the Gerhold Players.

He wrote: 'The present producer of the Gerhold Players has somewhat reduced the intrusive rawness that was associated with this group. Yet he and the cast will have to do some hard study before their presentations can approach the standards of, for instance, the Amherstian Players.' Actually, Peter was a good trouper and a welcome performer on stage, especially with his monologues.

He may have been a bit out of his depth as a play producer, or was the critic expecting too much from the amateur stage?

Abortionist charged with murder of girl aged 17

READERS of the *Evening Press* on 1 March 1943 were shocked to learn that Benjamin Brunt, who since the Occupation had practised as a chiropractor, had been arrested by police and charged with the murder of a 17-year-old girl following an illegal operation.

Brunt came to Guernsey shortly before the Occupation, accompanied by his wife, evidently to purchase cattle. Instead, he opened up a business as a chiropractor and did well.

After his arrest, he was committed for trial before the Royal Court, which found him guilty, not of murder, but of manslaughter. By this time, two other charges had emerged but he was found not guilty of performing an abortion on another woman but guilty of supplying noxious pills or powder to a third. He was sent to prison for three years.

Brunt, who gave himself the title of doctor, was supported by his wife. She told the court that he had become a good, kindly husband and father. Accused told the court that he had been under pressure from the women to bring about abortions – one threatened to kill herself if she could not be helped.

It was unfortunate that Brunt became involved in such a practice because he had a good following of patients for his chiropractor business with many people convinced of his ability.

The Lyric Theatre Management was given permission by the Royal Court to run Sunday charity shows. The first to be staged would be in aid of the Red Cross Fund. It was stated that 'all the Lyric favourites' would be taking part.

On 3 March, the *Guernsey Press* carried the draft of a long order in connection with blacking out lights from buildings. The enemy wanted to ensure that there was no light issuing from any building that might help lead Allied aircraft to their targets. In special instances, dimmed blue lights would be permitted, such as in telephone kiosks.

■ GERMAN AIR POWER: A Luftwaffe Heinkel peeks out from a hangar at Guernsey Airport.

From Sark, came the timely news that the minute hand of the west clock in the tower of St Peter's Church had parted company with the rest of the works. Despite the absence of the Sark vicar, St Peter's Church was still holding services on Sunday mornings and afternoons on an alternate basis. Thanks were due to Dr Ibotsdon who, as a lay reader, was conducting the worship.

A workmen's kitchen at Berthelot Street continued to provide hot meals on Monday, Wednesday and Friday evenings. This was under the direction of the Dean of Guernsey, with Alice Collins taking the money from each table. Soup and vegetables cost 1s and for another 6d a liberal second helping could be provided. Some 55 men were attending and they were said to be mainly those who had been separated from their wives by the evacuation.

Growers in Guernsey were told that in order to comply with the cropping plan for 1943, they had to grow tomatoes. Those owning 500ft of glass or more should plant at least half the area in tomatoes and those with less glass than above, a reasonable proportion. Inspectors would be visiting properties to ensure that growers complied with the law.

The Bailiff, Victor G. Carey, had received a letter from Frank Stroobant, who was in Germany. He was appealing for three or four footballs in order that soccer could be played in the camp, of which he was the senior leader. No doubt they were duly despatched.

A farmer in the north of Guernsey was very perplexed. One of his cows had produced a creature that seemed to be a cross between a pig and a heifer. It weighed 55lb – the normal weight of a newborn calf – but the legs were short and stumpy like those of a half-grown pig. There was a suggestion that the mother cow had been frightened by a pig while carrying her offspring. But the farmer declared that she had never been near a pig.

The Regal Players broke all previous records when they presented Ghost Train. A grand total of 5,292 people saw the play. From the proceeds of this record box office, the sum of £210 went to charity.

The 'Grand Old Man' of Guernsey Printing

THE death of Gervase F. Peek, described in a headline as 'Grand Old Man of Guernsey Printing World', was fully detailed in the edition of the *Evening Press* on 31 March 1943. He had recently celebrated his 88th birthday but had been unwell since Christmas.

As a builder, he erected many important buildings in the island, including a masonic hall, later becoming closely involved with leading island firms. For instance, he was chairman of the Guernsey Press Company Ltd. He worked extremely hard to improve island life. The *Press* stated that he was one of the best known and esteemed men in the Channel Islands. The funeral was held at St James-the-Less and a large number of people attended the service.

In Jersey, a man who had been described as the 'Napoleon of the Black Market' escaped from prison where he had been serving a sentence for illegal trading. The *Press* said he made his escape by 'jumping over the wall of the prison'. How high the

■ TWO DAYS: Some islanders were advised to leave their homes because of the Germans' practice firing of their big guns.

wall was is not recorded. Anyway, he fractured his two ankles in the attempt and was soon caught hiding in stables near the prison.

Readers of the *Press* on 24 March 1943 were warned that gunfire would shatter the peace of Guernsey for two days – 25 and 26 March. This meant that during the practice firing, some homes would be considered in the danger zone and the occupants would have to evacuate to safe districts. It seemed that the Germans were going to have a jolly old blast with their heavy weapons which, so far as the coastal batteries were concerned, did not see much proper action. Where some of the evacuees went is not recorded, but I suppose most stayed with relatives.

Hundreds of people had applied to the States for new cycle tyres and it was announced that a small number had arrived from France. Permits to purchase would be given to workmen needing to cycle to work and also people on essential duties. No further applications could be entertained at present but it was hoped that a further consignment would arrive sometime in the future.

Hubert Nicolle, who was a POW, having been detained by the Germans while on a spying mission to Guernsey, sent much needed medical supplies to the island in March 1943. Dr E. V. Gibson received the valuable parcel and handed it over to the Emergency Hospital at the Castel. The *Press* added that this was the first time that such Red Cross supplies had reached the island in

'It seemed that the Germans were going to have a jolly old blast with their heavy weapons'

such a way. The drugs and dressings would be a very welcome addition to present medical supplies.

In Jersey, tree planting was proceeding apace. A big reafforestation programme was under way, with many thousands of young saplings being purchased by the States

14

from local nurseries. The plan was not only to plant trees where others had been felled but also to improve areas of the island, which had lain barren for years.

Some horses had been imported into Guernsey by the States and four were put up for auction. They fetched a total of £1,035, which was considered to be very good.

Mrs Betsy Sauvarin was about to celebrate her 100th birthday. She had been able to read up to a year ago but her eyesight was failing, which also prevented her from knitting. The *Press* asked a relative if there would be a celebration but they were told that such excitement would be too much for Betsy. She lived at Le Rocher, Gele Road, Castel in one of the most picturesque cottages in the island. A few friends called on her during the day.

A letter writer observed that an instance of longevity had been published recently. Out of five deaths, there were three of over 90 years and a fourth of 76 years.

'This is not withstanding that we have been mostly on a vegetable diet for nearly four years.' The letter writer thought that this might well be a record.

British blamed for shortages

THE Germans tried to ram home to Channel Islanders in April 1943 that nuisance raids by the British forces would be to blame if there were shortages of supplies. They issued a notice stating that in all areas they occupied, a supply of foodstuffs had been maintained.

However, the British military command, disregarding the fact that Channel Islanders were their own countrymen, were attempting in every way to jeopardise the continuous supply to the islands through raids.

'If, in consequence of these raids, the rations of islanders have now to be decreased, the population can thank for this their own countrymen on the other side of the Channel,' said the German notice. 'Churchill and his supporters will not achieve any military success from such nuisance raids. But it characterises their notorious lack of scruples that they do not refrain from exposing their own fellow countrymen to sufferings that could be avoided.

'The population of the islands, however, may at least know their culprits.'

An order during the month informed islanders that they had to apply to the German authorities before beginning new building projects. Failure to do so could result in a fine being imposed or imprisonment.

There was an unusual application made to the Royal Court.

A girl sought the appointment of a guardian who would permit her to marry as she was under age and her widowed mother had been evacuated.

The court granted the application, which was probably unique in the island's legal history.

Rats were proving a menace in Guernsey.

With less food about, the vermin were said to be turning to new crop potatoes in the fields, digging them out of the ground. Farmers were given permission to do their own digging in order to conserve stocks for humans. The Rat Destruction Department was very busy, calling on properties to help owners to control the pests. Glasshouse sites were particularly attractive to the vermin.

Incidentally, the Amherstian Players were presenting the play, 'Well Caught, at the Lyric' – I don't think it had anything to do with rats.

Butchers were asking their customers to collect their meat ration as there was a shortage of men to deliver it. Also, they should bring their own paper in which to wrap the meat.

The Island Stores in Sark was broken into, but the thief did not get much of a haul – just one cigar.

Evidently, it was non-ration week for tobacco so stocks were rather low.

Off duty, the German soldiers in Guernsey had a wide range of interests. Football, games of skill, chess, painting and carving all came within their ambit.

Le Cheminant's, the photographer in the Arcade, put on a display of German paintings and carvings selected at random from the items in a recent exhibition.

One of the paintings, a Guernsey coastal scene, was reproduced on the front page of the *Press* of 9 April.

There was somebody who was definitely not hungry – the thief who broke into La Moye Stores, Vale and got away with weekly rations for 150 customers, including 59lbs of butter and fats, coffee, sugar, beans and other commodities.

A quantity of knitting wool had become available and applications were invited by the States. Expectant mothers could make special application for quantities of white wool with which to knit baby garments.

Tar was becoming a useful commodity. Householders came to realise that when mixed with cinders and coal dust, it made the best possible fuel for open fires. Once mixed, it would be deposited on an existing fire and left to cake for some two hours. Once the surface of the mix was broken, the fire flared up – it is hoped not halfway up the chimney.

The *Press* stated that such fires lasted for hours and the

cinders could be reclaimed for further mixes. The tar cost 8d a gallon.

Hundreds of islanders were now going over to this method of heating their home.

There was disappointment for bus users. The services from Town each morning were discontinued until further notice. In future, the first bus to leave St Peter Port on all routes would be the 12.30pm.

The decision was due to 'unforeseen circumstances'.

Bringing local news to CI deportees

THERE was news in April 1943 that the *Guernsey Evening Press* was arriving regularly at camps where Channel Island deportees were living. The newspapers were always in great demand. A letter from Frank Stroobant, who was camp senior at one of the internment camps on the Continent, was sent to the Bailiff and duly published. It indicated that general conditions were good and education of all standards was on offer.

At a meeting of the States of Deliberation, the sum of £1,050 was voted as an additional amount to cover the work of St John Ambulance for 1943. The House was told that the work of the service had increased considerably and this would continue. St John had a call to remove a woman to hospital for treatment. Her son climbed a wall to watch the removal from her home, but as the ambulance was leaving, the youth fell and fractured his left forearm.

■ DEPORTEES: The working party for the Red Cross and YMCA at Laufen, 1942-5; Frank Stroobant, who wrote to the Bailiff about camp conditions, is seated on the far right.

In those days there was no radio control for the ambulance service so it could not be called back. On arrival at hospital, the mother was quickly unloaded the ambulance returning to her home to pick up her son.

Auxiliary police officers were also required. They had to be between 20 and 35 and of good physique, education and appearance. The minimum height was 5ft 8in and they had to be in possession of a bicycle equipped with a dynamo and knowledge of French would be an asset. The pay would commence at £2 14s 3d per week plus allowances.

The *Evening Press* of 21 April carried the picture of a special stamp marking Hitler's birthday. He was 54 the previous day and the stamp bore a picture of the evil man.

Since the start of the Occupation, a working party at St Martin's had been busily engaged in making clothing, especially for children. But now old garments for cutting up to make new were getting very short. The group therefore used the *Press* to appeal for more material with which to work.

The *Press* reported that field mice were invading homes, seeking food. However, they seemed to be avoiding bait placed in traps. Householders were asking the authorities for advice on avoiding yet another occupation.

Many islanders will remember when Harry W. Ingrouille was the talented organist at St Joseph Roman Catholic Church. It was reported in April 1943 that he had become the organist when only 16 years old and had now reached 21. He offered a programme of music in the church. The *Press* commented that Harry was a zealous student.

For those inclined, sport and entertainment were obtainable in various forms and rugby was fast gaining favour.

It was with particular interest that I read a report in a German Occupation issue of the *Press* of an oil painting which had been produced by Arthur Selous with whom I worked. He had reached professional standards and had agreed to make a copy of the ill-fated brigantine, Rescue, which had been under the command of Captain Samuel Winterflood, my greatgrandfather.

The original painting had hung in the office of the late Peter Dorey, who managed the firm of Onesimus Dorey in the Pier Steps. He kindly loaned the picture so that Arthur could make the copy, again in oils, and present it to my grandfather, the late Captain Charles Winterflood, who had sailed in the vessel.

The painting came to me and is now hanging in the home of my son, Stephen.

Initially, it caught the eye of a reporter when it was on display in the shop window of the Singer Sewing Machine Co. in Smith Street. The reporter interviewed my grandfather but got his Christian name wrong. It was not David, but Charles, who was then 84. He had sailed in the Rescue during the 19th century and recalled that the ship was built at St Sampson's. The first company ran out of cash and the vessel was completed by Onesimus Dorey. Being thus rescued financially, it was appropriate to call her the Rescue.

On her maiden voyage to London, she had most of her canvas blown away and my grandfather broke an arm. Eventually her life ended when she struck a rock off the Nore, was rammed by a following vessel, sank and two of the crew drowned. In German Occupation days, it was impossible to get proper painters' canvas so Mr Selous executed his skill on canvas from a deck chair.

21

Keeping up appearances

THE German notice, which appeared at the end of April 1943, informing Channel Islanders that British Forces had been carrying out nuisance raids, which would have repercussions in the islands in respect of essential supplies, was followed on 3 May with an article about fish supplies.

It emphasised that the fair distribution of fish had become more important than ever. Fish would be a welcome addition to the larder, especially in summer months. In the past, people had complained bitterly about methods of distribution – not without foundation, according to the *Press*.

Ernest Stead had been appointed Fish Controller and he would have wider powers than his predecessor. He promised that he would do all in his power to ensure that fish was evenly distributed. The controller said that there had been too much under-the-counter selling and preference given to certain customers. This had to go.

The new order demanded that all fish allocated to retailers had to be displayed on their stalls. If there was doubt about this, Mr Stead had the power to search the stall and he said he would do this if he felt it necessary. Part of the new order also enabled the controller to sell fish himself if the retailer was not present and there was fish on the stall and people waiting to be served. Mr Stead told the *Press* that he was taking his job very seriously and would attempt to remove racketeering from the industry.

At the beginning of May 1943, two families had to quickly escape from their homes in the Ruette Braye district. Fire destroyed the two houses and damaged a third. Both Guernsey and German firemen turned out and were on the scene within four minutes of the call. But, by this time, the fire had gained a strong hold on both properties and both structures collapsed as the firefighters arrived. They saved the third house but had to spend more than three hours at the scene.

Some boot polish – black and brown – had arrived in Guernsey and islanders were invited to 'rise and shine'. The

LYRIC THEATRE General Manager: PETER CAMPBELL

SECOND ANNIVERSARY
SOUVENIR PROGRAMME

WE
THREE

PETER CAMPBELL **FOUNDERS** ERIC SNELLING

FRED WILLIAMS
(Late Manager)

now

absent from the

Island.

1942 **1944**

Monday, 10th January, 1944
For Six Evenings, with Thursday Matinee

PRESS LTD.

■ LOSING FAVOUR: The Lyric Theatre closed for one week to maintain its entertainment standards after audiences walked out midway through a show.

23

polish could be purchased for 1s 7d (large tin, brown only) and 1s 3d (small, black and brown). In order to get future supplies, empty tins had to be supplied to the retailers for onward delivery to the manufacturers. Buyers were asked to co-operate for their own sake.

Some chocolate had also arrived and under-14s could obtain a ration of five bars from retailers supplying them with sugar. The States Water Board put a ban on the use of hoses for watering gardens. Islanders were sorry to read that the bread ration was to be reduced. Heavy workers, male and female, would get a little more than the rest of the population. One woman put a small ad in the *Press* requesting that people who were spreading rumours about her 'to stop it'.

Bill Green was evidently getting bogged down with cycle repairs in May 1943. He placed an advertisement telling customers that he was not opening his Smith Street shop on Mondays. His staff would work behind closed doors to keep up with the task of keeping the population on two wheels. In a tape recording made before his death, he paid tribute to his employees who had worked hard on the repair of bikes at a time when there were few spare parts.

The Lyric Theatre management decided for one week not to stage entertainment. General manager Peter Campbell explained that every effort had been maintained to keep to a good standard. Recently a show had been staged, which had not found favour with audiences. Some had walked out midway through. It had therefore been necessary to adopt a firm policy to ensure that standards would be maintained in future. There had been previous complaints in the *Press* about theatregoers arriving late for performances. The Regal Players evidently took note and made it known that latecomers would not be admitted until the end of the first act.

Sark Chief Pleas met to appoint La Dame as Acting Dame de Sercq. She would act in place of her husband who was no longer in the island. One deputy questioned this but was told that all Sark officials could appoint a deputy in their absence.

Avoiding falling shrapnel

ISLANDERS were warned to keep their heads down and prepare for emergency when air raids were in progress. The names of companies that were providing air-raid shelters were given and people were advised to stay put once they had taken cover.

Those allowing their selfish curiosity to bring them into the open during raids should realise that, if they sustained injury, others would have to endanger their lives by coming to the rescue. This warning was partly prompted by an incident a little earlier in May 1943 when three locals were hit by flying shrapnel. When most of the anti-aircraft guns opened up in Guernsey, the shrapnel used to fall like hailstones.

One evening I was attending a film performance at the Gaumont when the guns fired at a British or American plane. Down came the shrapnel onto the roof of the cinema causing quite a disturbance. We boys used to comb the fields after such

■ DANGEROUS: Islanders were warned to stay undercover during air raids.

firing trying to find the biggest pieces of shell possible. All specimens were very jagged and dangerous when falling from a great height. Pity the poor glasshouses.

With longer daylight hours, the Germans decided that they could allow civilians in the streets until 11pm. This allowed dances and other entertainment to start later. Alan Jory, organiser of the Island Ballroom Championships, was pleased with the success of the event and of the money raised for charity.

However, he expressed disappointment that some of the people interested had been unable to see it because of the size of the hall available. Shows at Candie were soon due to start for the summer. It was proposed to improve the comfort of patrons by installing at least 60 tip-up armchairs. Eventually, it was hoped that the 800 seats would be of this type and cushioned. The buffet and cycle park would again be available. During the previous season, 20,000 drinks were sold and 3,629 cyclists used the parking facilities.

A new scheme for butter-milk distribution was worked on by the States Dairy. It had not been made available because of the quantity being produced. The ration would be less than one-third-of-a-pint per person.

People hoping to buy spider crabs in the Market took part in a protest as they faced two chests containing the crabs. They did not want to give up their ration coupons for the crabs, preferring to go home and wait for wet fish. The stallholder said he would put the crabs on display and if they did not sell, he would put in a claim to the States. The next day, an official order exempted spider crabs from the rationing system.

The potato ration was increased to 5lb per week per head. This was instead of the previous 3lb of outdoor-grown potatoes available, having the advantage of very little waste.

By now, various growers were cultivating tobacco plants and it was thought that there would be a good sale for the leaves. Growers were advised to allow the harvested leaves to dry off in glasshouses for about four weeks. To ferment, the bunched leaves should be left on the floor and turned regularly. It was further stated that tobacco leaf production in Jersey was more common than in Guernsey and large areas were now planted out. A hard-working housewife wrote a letter to the *Press* concerning controlled prices. She suggested that islanders were supposed to have the benefit of it, but she suggested that such legislation could be evaded. She further suggested that controlled prices were driving people away from the shops and direct to growers. Her argument was that under-the-counter sales were further developing and that people receiving standard wages had to limit purchases to potatoes, cabbage and lettuce. She further alleged that the system favoured the well-to-do, who could afford to pay extra for their food. The writer asked if something could be done about this.

Controlled prices lead to uncontrolled complaints

I HAVE a sneaking feeling that the civilian authorities in Guernsey during June 1943 wished that they had never introduced price control. A right royal battle developed between people with different involvements – the producers, the retailers and the public.

Letters to the editor of the *Guernsey Press* poured in and there seemed to be no end to the problem. The fact that the Germans were occupying the island was almost forgotten as people put

■ FISHY ISSUE: The Dame of Sark told a Chief Pleas meeting in 1943 that fishermen must stop selling fish directly instead of sending it to the Guernsey market.

pen to paper to protest. It had started with a woman writing regarding the price control and this was enough to stir most of the island's civil population.

The States had introduced a maximum price list for a wide range of products, but it was felt that producers were keeping foodstuffs back from retailers and selling it at higher prices direct to the public. The producers said that, due to the high cost of production, the maximum price permitted was too low. Retailers were accused of keeping goods under the counter for special customers and they also complained at the restrictions on what they could charge.

I dread to think what would happen today if the States attempted to introduce similar legislation. What was alleged to be happening could be proved by watching reports from the police court where people were summoned for overcharging.

For instance, on 2 June 1943, a report was published about a grower overcharging for cucumbers. He should have asked 1s 8d for four pounds but instead charged 3s 4d. Unfortunately, the purchaser was a police officer in plain clothes. The grower was fined £2 and ordered to refund the excess amount.

From early June, the letters flowed in to the editor's desk and more growers and traders faced court appearances for what was described as 'under-the-counter sales'. Then came a report, in the form of a letter, in which growers drew up their own price list and made a case for changing the controlled charges.

A long list of suggested revised prices were given – in some instances only 6d more, in other cases, rather heavier. Some increases varied with the season. The price for strawberries was given as: forced, 10s per pound up to 31 May; outdoor, 5s per pound throughout the season.

Presumably, the problem continued in the ensuing months of 1943, but we must wait and see when the pages of the *Press* are further turned.

At the Sark Chief Pleas, La Dame told the gathering that she had received information that not enough fish was being sent to Guernsey for sale. She said that more had to be sent to the Guernsey market and selling direct by fishermen must stop. The meeting continued until 9.50pm when one member reminded the gathering that the curfew was at 10pm. The members then rose en bloc and, while standing hastily, agreed to the law that bread must be weighed in front of customers buying from shops. Everybody then jumped on their bike and tried to reach the safety of their homes before the fatal hour struck from the church clock.

The church clock was mentioned in the first court hearing of an alleged curfew infringement. Mr and Mrs H. H. Lanyon, the island's baker and storekeeper and his wife, were reported for being out after 10pm. But Mr Lanyon maintained that the church clock had registered 9.58pm when they were stopped. He thought something should be done about ensuring that the clock was kept at the correct time. The court agreed but nevertheless fined the Lanyons £1 each for infringing the curfew law.

'There seemed to be no end to the problem. The fact that the Germans were occupying the island was almost forgotten as people put pen to paper to protest'

The States Committee for the Destruction of Rats issued a statement about the increasing rodent population. Two men were solely employed on rat destruction, but islanders often did not call for assistance until considerable damage or financial loss had been experienced. People were urged to make war on the rat population. They could still obtain the necessary poison at chemists.

In June, the Gaumont Cinema screened the film 'Racketeers of the Range' – there were no local stars appearing. For 6d, islanders could enjoy an orchestral concert at Candie Gardens. This was courtesy of the Santangelo Orchestra on a Sunday evening.

Fishermen caught more than they bargained for

TWO Guernsey fishermen lost their lives and two more cheated death when a mine exploded near the boat they were using. The accident happened north of Herm and those killed were Herbert Dunn, 21, and Archibald Sebire, 28. Brothers John and Harry Quinain lost their boat and equipment, but were grateful to have survived.

The explosion happened when the fishermen were hauling in a bobber. Another craft managed to reach the survivors and took them aboard. A fund was immediately started for the fishermen. Both the *Evening Press* and the *Star* newspapers each gave £5 to launch the fund and by the end of June, £1,298 had been raised. It was stated that some of the cash would help the Quinain brothers replace their boat.

In other news, it was decided to export tomatoes to France and growers were told that they would receive 4s 5d for each first-grade 12lb chip, reducing as the season progressed. There would also be a second grade, whites, but all fruit had to be in a hard condition for travelling. Of course, this created jobs for the men and women. The former were needed to manage tomato depots throughout the island and the latter for tomato picking.

A 2lb jar of Hartley's marmalade had been offered to the highest bidder, with the money going to the Red Cross Society in appreciation of its work. Thinners were being advertised for in a bid to save a grape crop. Good wages would be paid on an hourly basis.

Paul Le Moal, who joined the *Guernsey Evening Press* in 1909, received and accepted an invitation to join the board of directors in June 1943. He was described as 'one of the most accomplished craftsmen of the printing trade in Guernsey'.

The police arrested three young foreign workers after a hunt lasting several weeks. It was alleged that they had been involved in a series of thefts. A civilian gave information to a constable, which resulted in a watch being kept on the men's

■ UNUSUAL VIEW: An interesting photograph appeared on the front page of the *Guernsey Evening Press* on 4 June 1943. It showed Sark's Creux Harbour with German boats unloading supplies. The island was described as 'the most lovely pearl in the necklace of the romantic Channel Islands'.

hideout. The arrest was made without any violence.

Frank Le Lacheur, 65, of Rosaire Avenue, St Peter Port was out for a walk with his invalid wife when both were attacked by a bull in Mount Row. Both were pushed over. The animal had escaped from Havilland Hall and it was lucky that a resident of Mount Row came to the assistance of the couple. The husband sustained cuts and bruises and his wife was suffering from shock. She was being pushed in an invalid chair.

There was now a pressing need for nurses uniforms at the Town Hospital (now the police station). The Hospital Board therefore appealed for material that would be suitable for making them. It was also hoped that some people might possess uniforms they would be willing to donate to the cause.

On 30 June 1943, people were told that an islandwide water curfew would be introduced the following day. The prohibited hours would be from 10pm until 5am. Some parishes would be cut off entirely during these hours. Where it was not possible for the authorities to disconnect the supply, the regulations had to be observed.

You could now buy purified carrageen moss collected from our beaches. An advertisement claimed that the moss was nourishing and satisfying and could produce delicious jellies. It was being sold for 1s a packet by C. Stonelake and W. H. Davies, the chemists. A trial of this product would convince.

A housewife complained bitterly in the *Guernsey Press* about stallholders in the fish market opening up too late in the day. She considered that 9am was far too late to start business and that they should ensure an opening hour of 7am. The woman claimed that she had been told that, in times of peace, old women had been seen shelling peas at 3.30am at Covent Garden. The writer urged fishmongers to take up the burden of the war and start selling early, thus saving busy mothers from endless queuing.

33

German guns on guard

'GERMANY'S Hold on the Channel Islands' was the headline over a photograph on the front page of the *Press* on 2 July 1943. The picture showed a German gun and crew ready for action at the lookout at the Blue Mountains. Before them stretched the harbour of St Peter Port. The story below quoted from a news announcement from Bremen and stated that the Germans had been occupying the Channel Islands for three years.

'The islands are now bristling with weapons against any form of attack: Guernsey especially being strengthened in the matter of the power of gunfire and joining with the Continent in showing resistance to any invasion from the Atlantic. Indeed, the power of German gunfire in Guernsey has been put to the test on occasion when British vessels, apparently attempting to effect a landing, were met by the fire of heavy guns.

'Guernsey's capital still contains 17,000 persons, the remainder having fled. The German troops are guarding to prevent any recapture of the island.'

I leave it to you to make what you can of the above propaganda. A few days later, there was a picture of one of the German observation towers. The location was not given, but I think it was the one facing south at Pleinmont.

From now on, more pictures were appearing in the *Press*, some showing groups of internees in Germany, some of current residents and, of course, battle scenes, especially from the Russian front.

The German newspaper, published in Guernsey for the benefit of the occupying forces, was celebrating its first birthday. More than 300 issues of the *Deutsche Guernsey Zeitung* had gone out. Islanders were informed that the next issue would be a lavish one with a special article marking the third anniversary of the German arrival in the island. It would be headed: 'Three Years' Watch on the Channel'. The Germans had ordered that all boats be removed from the Castle Emplacement to sites inland.

This job was undertaken by the Civil Transport Service under the direction of Mr E.W. Laker. He had a group of six men and they were engaged for some time in getting all the craft cleared. One problem was the lack of special equipment that was usually available for such an operation.

There were no busy bees in Guernsey in July 1943. The *Press* carried a report stating that they had not been very active. Evidently a persistent northeasterly wind made conditions unfavourable for the production of nectar in plants. The number of bee swarms was exceptionally low.

One consolation: there was a meat ration promised for the week.

The Town Hospital had been advertising for nurses uniforms and aprons and there had been a good response. Complete uniforms had been offered. Some had been paid for, but not at ridiculous prices. The Town Hospital seemed to be satisfied for the present, but islanders were asked to remember others who could be in need.

On 7 July, a picture appeared showing the German Orchestra giving an open-air concert at Cambridge Park. An interview with the bandmaster, Gerhard Anders, accompanied the photo.

The edition of the *Press* for 9 July devoted a long article to the Brache sisters. The headlines gave their Christian names as Freda and Daphne and their father played the piano. The heading also revealed that the sisters were discovered at a Northern ARP concert.

The reporter asked if islanders had remembered an act at the Regal two years previously when two demure young ladies walked onto the stage and sang in that mischievous manner: 'And

'We were five to six minutes away from the explosion and did not think that anybody had survived. However, as we drew near the scene, I saw an arm in the water'

Lloyd Le Conte

35

then the lights went out'. Since then, they had become one of the most popular variety turns on the Guernsey stage. The man who discovered the act was Peter Campbell, who attended the ARP concert at St Sampson's. He heard them singing with others in the hall and decided that they were better than those on stage.

'The Germans insisted that two people had to be in each fishing boat'

Sark saved the day for fish supplies on 9 July. It sent 15cwt of lobsters, dogfish, ray and whiting to the Guernsey Fish Market.

The Germans took obvious delight in printing pictures of badly damaged Cologne Cathedral after Allied air raids. The German-controlled press described the raids as 'terror attacks', the headline being 'Military Objective!'

We had not been shown damage to civilian areas of Britain. There was a claim that so far in the Second World War, the British had eradicated more than 500 European churches.

In Jersey, firemen were busy tackling furze fires. During one weekend three had to be quelled.

Following last month's second instalment of "Occupied Guernsey", mention was made of the boating accident off Herm in June 1943 when Herbert Dunn and Archibald Sebire died after a mine, which they pulled up in their nets north of Herm, exploded. Brothers John and Harry Quinain, who were also in the boat, survived. One of the men who went to their rescue was Lloyd Le Conte, who was fishing with Dan Domaille in the Marina GU56.

'I went out with him as the Germans insisted that two people had to be in each fishing boat,' explains Lloyd. 'We were five to six minutes away from the explosion and did not think that anybody had survived. However, as we drew near the scene, I saw an arm in the water. We managed to pull both the Quinain brothers to safety.'

Both explained how they had gone under water for a

36

considerable depth and wondered if they would ever surface again. Lloyd and Dan were stopped from fishing for three days while the Germans questioned them.

'The Germans thought that we were telling them lies about the accident because we had not returned with boat wreckage. They were suspicious that the two missing men had, in fact, travelled off to the UK in their boat. But we explained that we were not bothered about bringing wreckage back to Guernsey,' said Lloyd.

It is obvious that the brothers had a very lucky escape in more than one sense. Soon after the accident, fog came down and then there was no way of locating the area of the explosion. It was reported that the brothers did not take money offered to them from a specially launched fund, preferring to give their share to the two families of the missing men. This was because they had a second boat.

Living in a minefield

DESPITE the fact that a young man had been killed by entering a minefield, islanders seemed still to be ignoring German notices warning of the danger.

At Bordeaux, a man gathering rabbit food in July 1943 had his right foot blown off. He managed to drag himself to safety and was attended by St John Ambulance staff. The *Guernsey Press* stressed the need to heed the warning notices, as not to do so would put the lives of rescuers in danger.

In Jersey, 300 workers were being sought to dig the island's potato crop. Even part-timers were welcome.

On 14 July 1943, the *Press* announced that it was to be a meatless week. Therefore the new fish control scheme would have a good test. Controller Ernest Stead explained that his scheme involved shopping to a timetable.

On Friday morning the Fish Market would be closed; then it would open from 2pm until 3.30pm. Coupons from one to three only would be valid. From 3.30pm onwards, coupons four and five would become valid. There would be a lunch hour for fishmongers.

The controller said he had invented this scheme in order to avoid unnecessary queuing up.

Tomato exports from Guernsey to France had reached destinations safely. Cargoes of 30,000 to 40,000 packages had been leaving the island regularly.

The Germans wanted to know in advance of any plans to make charitable appeals or collections. This did not apply to those being taken in churches during divine worship.

In conjunction with the civilian authorities, the Germans issued a notice in July 1943 to the effect that stern measures would be taken over the pricing of goods above the recognised amounts. This also included black market activities. People were urged to report any such instances. Law breakers could discover that their businesses would be closed down if they were found guilty of an offence of overcharging.

Dorothy Hurrell was packing the Central Hall with her dancing displays. It was said to be a fast-moving show with no waits between performances. The *Press* carried a photograph of a young Miss Hurrell. A German critic was delighted with the solo dancing by Dorothy.

Mary Toms, herself an entertainer, was advertising for good spare time knitters at her shop premises at 20 Commercial Arcade.

Many rabbits being reared in Guernsey were dying because of the disease spotted liver. The *Press* issued a report stating that rabbits were still edible and suggested that nobody would be foolish enough to kill sick rabbits for consumption – not even in these times of food shortage.

At Candie Gardens, Edward Le Huray was presenting 'The Rogues', a concert with an attractive programme.

I don't think the title had anything to do with people who seemed bent on breaking the law by charging over the controlled price for goods.

'The Press issued a report stating that rabbits were still edible and suggested that nobody would be foolish enough to kill sick rabbits for consumption'

Expectant mothers were warned that the white wool reserved for them so they could knit clothes for their expected arrivals was running out. In future, they would have to make do with a maize-coloured wool.

The *Press* found it necessary to issue the following notice during July 1943.

'Advertisers who make use of the classified columns should note that we are no longer accepting advertisements offering for sale or exchange, or asking for goods that are rationed or controlled.

'Such articles as sugar, flour, butter, cigarettes, etc. have been deleted from advertisements; neither is it permissible to cover foodstuffs with the word commodities.'

On the same day the States issued an order banning the sale or exchange of pigs, goats, poultry or rabbits. People breaking the order could expect to be fined up to £100 or six months in jail or both. This also applied to the advertising of same for sale or barter.

The States wanted 10 women for sorting the island's potato crop as well as lads and girls for box factory work.

A quantity of woollen material had arrived from France and islanders were being invited to apply for same. It was said that the material could be used for the making of suits and overcoats for both men and women. The navy blue cloth would sell for 25s per yard and the blue/grey cloth would sell at 30s for the same amount.

How I remember my first long-trousered suit from France. It was dark blue with a white fleck. I spent hours looking down at my manly, long trousers. For work, I wore plus-fours converted by my mother into traditional trousers. The legs tended to go inwards in the ankle regions.

August saw exciting times

THERE was great excitement in the heart of St Peter Port on 5 August 1943. People in the Pollet and High Street scattered in all directions as a runaway horse careered through the streets. The horse and van had stopped in St Julian's Avenue when the animal was frightened. It bolted through La Plaiderie and, in the narrow thoroughfare, the back of the van jammed. But the horse broke loose, trailing the undercarriage, front wheels and shafts. The wheels came off in the Pollet and the horse continued at breakneck speed down High Street, eventually stopping in Fountain Street. The van was battered, but the horse appeared to have survived without a scratch.

Those were exciting days.

A children's allowance scheme was accepted by the States of Deliberation on 9 August 1943. It was limited to those dependent on the earnings of compulsory contributors of the contributory Pensions Law 1935 who were under school-leaving age and not at work as well as the children of widows in receipt of a pension under that law.

The rate of allowance was suggested to be 4s per child per week with provisos. The latter limited the earnings of dependants to, for instance, £3 with four children. Widows with four children would receive £2 9s.

The House voted £6,000 to cover the cost of the project.

At that time, the retail price of petrol was being increased to 5s 6d per gallon.

Besides dealing with injured islanders, the St John Ambulance Brigade was going into the realms of public entertainment. Through the brigade's social committee, a variety concert was being arranged entitled '70 Calling'. It would be staged at the Lyric and would be a non-stop show featuring well-known artists.

The Germans were advertising for three women for kitchen work. Quite a number of women did find such work in German kitchens. It was one means of earning a few more shillings and

■ OFF DUTY: German soldiers captured taking a cup of tea on a summer's day.

there was always the opportunity of coming home with a few extra snacks.

But some people were still forced to steal food; butcher E. W. James was offering a £5 reward for information relating to the theft of 50lb of beef from his stall in the Meat Market.

The *Guernsey Press* reported an accident that befell Deputy Wilfred Corbet, a well-known statesman. He was standing outside Les Camps Methodist Church after conducting a service there when he was knocked over by a car. He sustained abrasions to an arm and a leg and was treated by an ambulanceman who was nearby. A second man was also struck by the car and received a leg injury.

Also among the registered accidents for one week in August was the case of a woman who, while swatting flies, hit her hand against a door.

The Transport Authority was still involved in moving boats from the Castle Emplacement to sites inland. On 15 August, one large yacht 'foundered' at the Longstore. A wheel of the truck being used to convey it gave way. The heavy craft, named

Molin, was eventually moved but not without some difficulty.

Dr A. W. Rose lost a gold signet ring while bathing at La Vallette. He offered a £25 reward. Searches were made of the pool, which was drained for the purpose. But it was a young boy named Roger, who eventually collected the cash. He presented the ring to the doctor when he made a return visit to the pool to carry out another search.

Three people came before the court in August 1943 for gleaning wheat without permission from a field in the Castel. The Magistrate decided it was a serious offence and sentenced the three each to a month in prison, one week to be served at once and the remainder of the sentence deferred on defendants taking an oath to be of good behaviour.

A house was reported well alight at Mont Marche, Forest during the month. Local firemen turned out to the blaze as did the German Fire Service under the direction of an officer. The joint team spent over an hour tackling the outbreak, which left the house extensively damaged. It was a strange sight to see the fire appliance, Sarnia II, proceeding to fires with a mixed crew. The local firemen wore white-painted British-type helmets with the Germans using their own type of military one.

In for the long stretch

■ SIR AMBROSE SHERWELL: Who managed to gain concessions for islanders deported to Germany.

IT MUST be most unusual to go to church for your wedding and emerge on a stretcher.

But that was what happened to Freddie Bush and his bride, Kathleen Webber. Freddie was divisional superintendent of the voluntary section of St John Ambulance while his bride was a well-known nurse at the Emergency Hospital (now the Castel Hospital). As the couple emerged from the Castel Parish Church, and all in the name of fun, they were placed on stretchers and carried to their car under an archway of splints and officers canes. The medical-themed celebrations continued at a dance at the Emergency Hospital.

The *Guernsey Evening Press* in late August 1943 said that Guernsey had become an island of smallholders.

This was very true as any small piece of land capable of producing vegetables was snapped up for this purpose. A letter writer to the editor had not had much success with his allotment.

Birds and slugs had eaten his few strawberries and beans. His potatoes were affected by disease, with only 50 per cent of the crop edible, and he doubted if he would have more than three hundredweight.

The writer was disappointed to learn that in 1944 no seed potatoes would be available. He was afraid that if he and others used seed potatoes from a partly-diseased crop, the problem would spread further. He was thinking of giving up his garden as a useless proposition.

I can't say I blamed him. His letter was prompted by an official notice that in 1944 seed potatoes would be available only to farmers and others with large areas of land and not small allotment holders, who were urged to keep back their own spuds for use as seed.

The letter was followed by another from a market gardener who had at last done fairly well.

His first attempt at growing potatoes was not very successful so, before repeating the operation, he read up the horticultural details for a potato crop and next season obtained 600lb of healthy tubers from three perch.

From 18 August 1943, the Germans told islanders that they could not set foot on any beaches of the island. This revoked all permits for bathing or fishing from the shore. Permits for the gathering of seaweed remained valid.

Next came the order that all permits for fishing off Guernsey and Sark were withdrawn. It would be necessary to re-apply for permission to fish.

A few internees, who had been allowed back from Germany, gave accounts to the *Guernsey Press* on how they had worked and played in camp. One concession, which Mr A. J. Sherwill had managed to achieve, was walks under guard outside the camp lasting for three hours.

People in Guernsey were still charging over the regulated price for products. The offence took place in the vegetable market when a stallholder sold grapes above the price allowed. He was fined £5 with a deferred two-week imprisonment.

After three years spent in Guernsey and Jersey, Sdf. Kurt Goettmann left these shores. He was a member of the propaganda staff and his task was to issue world news to the local newspapers. As the front page of the newspaper filled each day with war news, he did not do too bad a job. He also had the task of screening subtitled German films at local cinemas and getting English-speaking films for local viewing.

The *Press* said that this German had been in contact with

many local artists and they found him helpful.

Horst Schmidt-Walkhoff arrived in the island as his successor.

The *Press* was again reporting the theft of produce from nurseries throughout the island. Amateur alarms were being fitted, consisting of string and bells, which would ring if intruders were not wary. At Bragg's flour depot at Glategny Esplanade, which was later in the Occupation used for Red Cross flour storage, string zigzagged the yard and, instead of bells, old cans were attached to the string. When St John Ambulance guard keepers arrived to relieve the nightshift, it was their job to clear the yard of the tins, only to be replaced at nightfall.

Weathering the storms

THE German Commandant issued a notice to Channel Islanders on 1 September 1943 to the effect that any person having in his or her possession guns, ammunition or hand grenades could now hand them in without any fear of being punished. However, they had to be surrendered by 15 September.

Meanwhile, a patron attending a concert at Candie Gardens wrote to the *Press* complaining at the noise being created by some people at the show. Evidently there was a lot of chat while performers were on stage. The writer suggested that the time to talk was between acts.

Another letter followed, suggesting that some of the noise would be avoided if the canvas flaps surrounding the auditorium were drawn closed.

These flaps were not ideal, causing noise in themselves during windy weather. After the war they were replaced by permanent glass partitions which made for much more comfort.

The *Press* was silly enough to report that a baby of 11 months had received his first haircut and asked: 'Could any child beat that?'

Well, once the edition was published, the phone in the editorial office began ringing with youngsters or their parents suggesting earlier haircuts. One was nine months and the other was eight.

I'm dreading to turn the next page of this file.

The front page of the *Evening Press* on 13 September 1943 carried banner headlines. They proclaimed that 'Germany is more resolute than ever before'. They were the words of Hitler, who also stated that neither time nor force of arms would cause the Reich to submit. In the course of his message, Hitler spoke of his personal grief over the way Mussolini was being treated and said he was happy to call the Italian leader his friend.

A great shame that he did not feel similar grief for the huge number of people who suffered degradation during his devilish reign.

On 12 September 1943, Guernsey experienced what was described in the *Press* as 'a freak storm'. Clouds began to gather in the heavens and islanders expected a downpour of heavy dimensions. Instead, the population was provided with a

■ ENTERTAINING THE TROOPS: Soldiers and islanders watch a German band play at Candie Gardens.

continuous lightning display. The brilliance in the sky was such that people declared that they had not seen the like before. At this stage not a drop of rain fell on Guernsey, but later in the night, teeming rain washed the streets.

Dr A. N. Symons, the medical officer of health for the States, decided to have yet another go at expectant mothers who left things until the last minute to call the ambulance. The doctor said that recently expectant mothers had left it until the night. This was not fair on the ambulance drivers and it was also a waste of petrol. In future women were urged to enter hospital during daytime for delivery.

St John Ambulance was busy in another field. It was running first aid courses for the injured. The course would last for seven weeks and both men and women would be welcome.

A picture of both Hitler and Mussolini appeared on the front page of the *Press* on 15 September. It was accompanied by a report giving details by the SS of the Duce's rescue from his captors in a mountain stronghold.

There was great jubilation in one of the German camps where Channel Islanders were held. For some time couples had remained separated, with the men in the camp for single people, but now they had been re-united with their wives. The report revealed that everybody was OK and all were happy about the reunion.

In the camps, there were sporting events and carnivals held over the August bank holiday and the proceeds – RM8,100 – were being divided equally between Guernsey and Jersey. The money was being sent to the Bailiffs of each island for the relief of distress or neediness. This was really a good show by groups of people held by Hitler as prisoners and who never knew what to expect from day to day.

Foundry closure threat as stocks run dangerously low

'ANY old iron?'

That was the call from the Channel Islands' only foundry in September 1943. For three years, Burgess Engineers Ltd, at Hougue a la Perre, Les Banques had been casting from its stock of iron and scrap metal. Now the company was down to its last ton.

It had used 200 tons since June 1940 to repair machinery in Guernsey and Jersey. John Upham, a director and general manager of the company, told the *Guernsey Press* that the need for more scrap metal was pressing. The company was appealing to islanders to come forward with any cast iron. It was prepared to collect the material. It was stressed that if iron was not forthcoming, then the foundry would close.

Nights were getting longer and the Germans decided to alter the curfew hours. Islanders would have to be in their homes by 10pm and would have to stay put until 6am. 'Kiddydrome', a dancing show by pupils of Joyce Ferguson, shattered attendance figures for wartime entertainment. The show, presented by Fred Leeder, had been staged for two weeks at Candie Gardens and had attracted an aggregate audience of 7,200.

Sark Court sat to hear a case involving a man who entered the grounds of La Seigneurie to kill and take a fowl. He denied the offence, but the court found him guilty and imposed a fine of 10s, plus 10s damages.

The German Commandant warned islanders again about the danger of wandering into minefields.

Following the registration of the new law regarding family allowances, payments were due to start being made from 25 September. Some 50 claimants had come forward seeking the weekly payment. However, many more applications were expected to be received.

Islanders were being urged not to use small potatoes for the making of flour, as this was considered wasteful. It was accepted that there were many small ones in the rations because of the island's poor potato crop in 1943.

A south-west wind late in September brought down apples from the trees. It also did the same for acorns. Gatherers were out collecting the acorns which had an economic value as they were used to make substitute coffee. Most of the churches appeared to be holding their harvest festival services on one Sunday – 12 September.

There was an opportunity for at least one woman to get on the right side of the law. The Royal Court House was advertising for a charwoman. More chocolate had arrived and would be available to young people of 14 and under and also to women of 15 and over. The ration consisted of 8oz of chocolate cream.

Local school life in 1943

BY OCTOBER 1943, the German authorities were weaving themselves closely within the framework of the civilian population.

For instance, the *Press* reported that Sonderfeuhrer A. Krefft had visited the States Intermediate School and had awarded special prizes to scholars who had shown good progress in learning the German language. The German visitor went to all the classes expressing the importance of learning a foreign language and adding that it would make their travelling more enjoyable.

A very nervous farmer was brought before the Magistrate's Court for failing to deliver to the States Dairy all the milk his animals produced. The court heard that the farmer was in the process of unloading cans at the dairy when firing started. This probably came from the anti-aircraft battery just behind it. Flustered, he made off with milk still in his vehicle.

He claimed he did not want it so he threw it away. However, he was fined £10, the Magistrate Jurat Quertier Le Pelley commenting that he did not consider the actions of the farmer were those of a sane man.

'I cannot understand his mentality,' said the Magistrate.

Complaints were flowing in from the public that grapes were being offered for sale in an unripe condition. This prompted Percy Dorey, president of the Glasshouse Utilisation Board, to warn growers to stop this practice. He issued an official order, which stated that bunches had to be of a reasonable size and berries must be sufficiently well coloured and must be ripe and sweet.

On the same day, it was announced that a further price control officer had been appointed to ensure that the order giving the maximum price for which goods could be sold was observed. Some women were infuriated by the way silk stockings from France were being distributed to islanders. Some traders satisfied bespoke orders leaving a non-existent supply

■ STOLEN RENAULT TANKS: One of the captured French tanks used by the Germans in Guernsey during the Occupation.

for others coming later. The authorities attempted to pacify the ladies by promising to introduce a more reasonable distribution system when the next supply of stockings arrived from the Continent.

Mr E. P. Rault from St Sampson's appealed to the parents of boys who had been evacuated from Les Vauxbelets College to hand in football shirts and stockings if still in their possession. These were needed for the wartime college being run by Brother Victor.

The team did not do very well when I played in it. They put me in goal against a St Martin's XI and I allowed 13 goals to be notched up by the opposing team. We scored none, which perhaps showed that it was not all my fault!

The Education Council was on the lookout for teachers to help instruct the 1,421 children needing to be educated. It was suggested that young ladies of good education might like to train as relief teachers. Archie Winterflood, secretary to the council, said that the relief teachers would work alongside trained teachers for six months to gain the necessary experience.

The States in October 1943 issued a list of imports from the Continent during the previous year. Oil and fuel formed the biggest items – almost £251,000 worth; clothing and footwear cost £87,000; wines and spirits £34,000; meat £26,495; and tobacco £28,000. Taking all trading with France into consideration, the total bill was more than £1m.

Ernest J. Baker, the 18-year-old son of E. T. Baker of Pollet Street, had just issued a stamp catalogue. The book contained a history of postal services in the islands since 1940, but people requiring a copy had to make haste to purchase as the supply was limited.

The money spent by States Committees in 1942 proved interesting reading. The Civil Transport Service spent £20,511 8s 8d with income being £20,999 0s 3d. The Farm Produce Board spent £12,770 3s 8d with income of £15,230 6s 9d. Public roads cost £8,992 5s 11d with an income of £18,047 3s 8d, which included tax on rental values.

Four schoolboys came before the Magistrate charged with stealing grapes from a private property. The Magistrate told all four that they could go, but if they came before him again for any offence, he would send them to prison to be birched.

The shows at Candie Auditorium had proved extremely popular with islanders. They had been run under the auspices of the Guernsey Entertainment Committee and during the summer of 1943 had attracted 75,000 patrons.

Editor forced to quit

A WAR on the rat population was undertaken by the German authorities midway through the Occupation. By 20 October 1943, the vermin population was rising rapidly and it was known that they were, and had become, a particular nuisance in vineries where they were devouring valuable food.

Supplies of poison were to be issued to the parish constables for them to dish out to ratepayers and it was hoped that this concerted effort would kill a large percentage of the rodents. All organisations and individuals concerned with rat-infested properties were being urged to join in the battle. One thing was certain: the Germans much preferred fighting rats in Guernsey than fighting on the Russian front.

With the nights darker for longer, cyclists were appearing in court for not using shaded headlights. The *Press* advised them that if they wanted to stay out of court, they should follow the blackout rules and shade their lamps, allowing just a horizontal aperture of light.

A youth aged 17, signing himself 'Indignant', sent this letter for publication in the *Press*: 'My pal, aged 14, is to have sweets; my brother, who is now one year my senior, has his ration of tobacco; my mother has chocolate and my granny, extra tit-bits.

'For how long must we boys between 15 and 18 continue to look and see the rest of the family enjoying themselves? Isn't it time that something was done for us, too?'

Needing to raise cash, the States introduced a tax on locally grown tobacco, production of which had increased significantly. It was hoped that £5,000 would be collected from the year's crop.

Press Editor Ken Gartell got into serious trouble with the Germans in 1943. A. A. Digard, chairman of directors of the *Guernsey Evening Press*, reluctantly issued the following statement: 'Mr K. Gartell will be dismissed from his office and cannot have any further connection whatsoever with the paper,

55

owing to his having come into conflict on several occasions with the German authorities at the Pressestelle.'

I say good for him, standing up as he did for his rights as an editor.

A farmer ended up in court for messing around with the milk that he produced for the States, having been seen to take a supply of four gallons into the Dairy and then leave with the same amount. A suspended sentence of one week in jail from a previous offence was imposed plus a fine of £10 or two months imprisonment.

Some church organs were going out of tune and the *Guernsey Evening Press* attempted to explain why.

The public was told that no local person could carry out certain tuning operations, so any improvement to the present sounds could not be remedied. People were asked to close their ears to any unfortunate sounding notes issuing from them.

In mid-October 1943, fishermen took 79 boxes of fish to the Market where some 90 people were in the queue at 9am and, to their joy, heard that 10 stallholders would be handling the fish.

The ration was 1lb per head.

One stall disposed of 1,825lbs of fish in 165 minutes to householders. This worked out at 11lb per minute. It was good to land the unexpected supply, most of it long-nose, because there was a meat ration.

The *Press* often carried medical reports of well known people who were in hospital. It was a nice touch.

Islanders mourned the hundreds lost at sea

NOVEMBER 1943 saw one of the most poignant periods of the Occupation. However, as Herbert Winterflood reports, some did their best for Guy Fawkes' Night and Christmas was coming too.

■ FULL MILITARY HONOURS: German forces burying British sailors who died when the cruiser, HMS Charybdis, and destroyer, HMS Limbourne, were torpedoed on 23 October 1943 in the Bay of St Malo. An estimated 4,000 islanders attended the service at the Foulon cemetery on 19 November, making it one of the Occupation's defining moments.

One of the saddest periods of the war for people living in Guernsey was during November 1943 when the bodies of British sailors were washed ashore.

More than 500 had died when HMS Charybdis and HMS Limbourne were sunk by enemy action in the Bay of St Malo. Inquests were followed on 19 November by the burial at the Foulon Cemetery of 21 seaman from HMS Charybdis.

The *Guernsey Press* estimated that about 4,000 people

attended the open-air service and 900 wreaths were sent. The German authorities gave the sailors full military honours, and it was indeed a most moving ceremony. The Bailiff, Victor Carey, laid a large wreath on behalf of the people of the Bailiwick.

At the conclusion of the service, we who attended were permitted to file past the graves in silent tribute. It was a scene never before witnessed in island history.

William Vaudin was appointed editor of the *Guernsey Press* on 3 November, replacing Ken Gartell who had annoyed the Germans. Because of his appointment, Mr Vaudin resigned as organist at St James-the-Less. His place was taken by Edgar Renier.

The authorities had evidently noted letters to the editor regarding young men of 14 and over not receiving a ration of chocolate. A new order permitted those up to the age of 17 to partake of the French chocolate.

A previous report in the *Guernsey Press* about organs not being able to be tuned brought a letter from Edward G. de la Mare, organ builder and tuner. He said that he and his staff could cope with all tuning needed. He further stated that if any pipe organs were defective, it was the fault of the authorities concerned with their upkeep.

Harry Till from the Pollet possessed a tandem but decided to convert it into a bicycle-made-for-three. It was about 10ft long and carried more than 30 stone. Eric Rabey made a tandem out of two cycles during the same period and I vividly remember borrowing the machine to take a girlfriend for a ride.

Guy Fawkes' day passed with little evidence that it had occurred. A few people donned masks and guys were set alight just before darkness fell to comply with German blackout regulations.

Hitler was on his soapbox again. In a speech, he declared that Germany would lay down arms only as victor. Retaliation would descend on Britain.

Six more men considered to be sick returned to Guernsey from internment in Germany.

A smash-and-grab raid in the Pollet livened things up for shop owner A. Machon. A large quantity of jewellery, including watches and rings, had been stolen.

So far 11 people had applied to be licensed tobacco cutters. Tobacco growing was becoming quite profitable and was now making money for the States through taxation.

The Water Department expressed the urgent need to conserve supplies. The *Guernsey Press* revealed that 90 million gallons held in reserve had been used up and more curfew restrictions on use might have to be introduced. A few days later, the threat was carried out. It was announced that the domestic supply would be cut off from 2pm to 5.30pm and from 8pm to 6am until further notice.

The St John Ambulance now had Christmas in mind and members of the social committee were asking for copies of specific carols for use at a service being organised.

Islanders were being advised to store roots for winter use. The Potato Board was now in a position to supply a range of root crops including carrots and swedes. This was an opportunity not to miss.

Two men appearing before the Magistrate were each fined 5s for riding their cycles without lights. At least they were not breaking the blackout regulations that hardly permitted any light up front. Perhaps just enough to see the kerb.

Le Cheminant, the toy shop, was still striving to stock goods, especially with Christmas approaching. It was advertising offering good prices for dolls, games, books and Guernsey-made toys.

Festive ration cheer

WITH Christmas approaching, an appeal went out for children's toys. Mrs Godfray Giffard of the Ozanne Hall Mission made the plea in November 1943 so that its children would not have their confidence shaken by not receiving gifts from Santa.

Tinned peas had arrived on the shelves of Guernsey shops in time for Christmas. The retail price per ration would total 2s 3d.

Women could eagerly await the arrival of Christmas. All over 18 were to receive a ration of 40 real cigarettes.

The States Electricity Department was in need of firemen, engine drivers and switchboard attendants. Applicants would be trained to fill such posts.

Some islanders in Jersey had a rude awakening in that month when an explosion rocked their district. A British mine that had been washed ashore unexpectedly exploded causing over £1,500-worth of damage. Several houses in the Fauvic and La Rocque area sustained damage from the blast. Surprisingly, nobody was injured.

On 20 November, a grand carnival dance was being held in St Martin's. It was the opening night of a series to be held at The Garage, Grande Rue. Dancing would be to the Premier Accordion Band, featuring Johnny Ferbrache and Roy Collins with Tommy Russell and his drums. Evening dress was optional and dancers could store their cycles free of charge.

Eighteen photographs of groups of internees in Germany had been received by the Bailiff. He handed them over to the *Press,* which promised to reproduce them at regular intervals in its journal.

The St John Ambulance was again inviting islanders to join its Invalid Transport Insurance Scheme. The minimum subscription was one shilling or half-a-mark.

The German bookshop in Smith Street was displaying books about the Channel Islands written by Germans themselves. These were illustrated, one picture showing La Grandemere at St Martin's Church. The *Press* suggested that this was one way of

■ LANDED: A German air force Junker 53 transport aircraft at Guernsey Airport during the German Occupation.

discovering how the Germans saw we Channel Islanders.

The death was recorded of one of the pioneer horse bus drivers, W. T. Watson, who had been in charge of one as far back as 60 years. He was employed firstly at Davey's Stables and later at the Perchard establishment. For many years, he drove the bus on the Town to St Martin's route.

As the growing of tobacco plants increased in Guernsey, the *Press* reminded its readers that such production occurred in the island during the 17th century. It was also an expanding crop in the UK so much so that the British production was proving a threat to the plantations in the USA. Therefore, in 1630, the Privy Council took action to prohibit tobacco growing in the UK and the Channel Islands. The authorities were ordered to destroy plants in the ground and to hinder future plantings.

On Saturday, 27 November 1943, the bodies of 40 officers and men of HMS Charybdis and a destroyer were buried in the German Military Cemetery at St Briene with full German military honours. The following day in St Malo, the captain, officers and ratings of Charybdis, numbering 102, were buried.

Fish controller Ernest Stead was doing his utmost to help housewives shop. He introduced a scheme whereby the women or others could contact the telephone operator at the central exchange to query if there was any fish available in the market. They would be told either 'yes' or 'no'. They were warned that they should not expect to be provided with a verbal list of the types available. The *Press* considered that this would be of great assistance to the hardworked housewives.

There was a thief about in St Martin's. The police reported that one householder had lost the majority of his rabbits, and in another instance, three fowls had been stolen.

Logs were now in great demand and trees became very valuable commodities. One tree owner was said to have made £125 from the sale of three large trees. The *Press* further reported that one buyer paid £25 for a tree, £5 to saw it up and £5 to cart it home.

I would have had a bit of an argument about that.

There were evidently pixies living in Guernsey in 1943. The *Press* reported that a pixie rain hood had been picked up in the Rohais some three weeks before but was still unclaimed.

Christmas with Germans

AND so we come to the last month of 1943 – and Christmas. It was perhaps difficult to understand the actions of the German nation at that time. Hitler and his cronies were involved in mass killings of innocent people yet on the front page of the *Evening Press* on 1 November was a picture of a Hitler Youth making toys for war orphans.

'Many a poor child will have a brighter Christmas, made possible by this splendid scheme,' read the caption.

Perhaps we were never intended to analyse the minds of individuals and nations at any given time in history.

The patients at the island's psychiatric hospital were being usefully employed. Under the direction of nurses, they were making slippers out of old felt hats.

From Sark came the news that Mr W. Giffard and family were leaving the island to take up residence in Guernsey. For nine years, Mr Giffard had taken charge of the Methodist Church and

■ COMMITTEE MEN: Members of the Wartime Controlling Committee.

had become one of the island's most popular personages. He would be remembered as president of the Sark Amateur Dramatic Society, a position he had held since its inception. He also produced plays and the *Press* said he would be greatly missed.

What was described as 'a detonation' foiled a thief who attempted to break into a house in the Vale. The noise, the source of which was not explained, awoke the householder and the would-be thief fled. Evidently, some tiny explosive device must have been operative in this home. The *Press* said that in order to make houses secure, islanders were adopting a Victorian habit of screwing the top half of windows to the lower half to ensure that they would remain shut against thieves.

On 4 December 1943, the funeral took place of yet another British sailor who had been washed onto an island beach. It was said that he was a member of the crew of HMS Charybdis. Full military honours were provided by the Germans. Leading island and German officials attended the service at Le Foulon.

'Perhaps we were never intended to analyse the minds of individuals and nations at any given time in history'

Also in that area, a thief broke into Harry Lihou's home and stole some clothing. It is recorded that on the following Sunday, Mr Lihou, who was a lay reader at St Stephen's Church, read as the appointed lesson: 'For know this, that if the good man of the house had known in what hour the thief would have come, he would have watched ...'

A few days later, Mr Lihou advertised in the *Press*, offering a reward to anybody finding a left Wellington boot in the Foulon area. Evidently the thief had taken only one such boot.

Organisation Todt wanted to pay its debts before Christmas arrived. It invited all firms with accounts outstanding to report to Saumarez Park where the amounts would be settled.

Internees in one of the camps in Germany were receiving excellent treatment to their teeth. Messrs S. H. Godfrey and S. G. Pay, both Guernsey dentists, were said to be doing marvellous work assisted by Mr Willis, a dental mechanic.

There would be no candlelight services in churches at Christmas. Essential Commodities announced that stocks of candles were almost exhausted and permits were no longer valid. Special permits allowing two candles a week would be reduced to just one.

Auctioneer A. J. C. Leech advertised a grand sale of presents, including toys for Christmas; this was one way of filling stockings.

A new magazine was to be launched in Guernsey. It would deal with life on stage and would cover news and views from the theatre. The editor would be W. H. Taylor, who was editor of *The Star*, which was also being published in Guernsey.

Little Sark had lost its last remaining horse and this created problems for the inhabitants. However, a tractor had taken over the task of carrying goods to and from the bigger section of the island.

More chocolate had arrived in Guernsey and a ration would be available before Christmas. Entitled would be young people aged 17 and under and women aged 18 and over. And there would be a ration of macaroni for all civilians. It began to look as if there would be something good on the table during the festive season, but the variety and amounts would be somewhat restricted.

Presents from Germany gave Christmas cheer

THREE hundred lucky people in Guernsey during Christmas 1943 were to receive chocolate from relatives and friends in a camp in Germany. A list of names to whom the gifts should go to accompanied the valuable packages, made up mainly of Rowntree's Plain York. The blocks each weighed a quarter of a pound. It was certainly a nice thought for those interned in Germany. Presumably the chocolate had been saved from Red Cross parcels delivered to the camp.

An appeal went out just before Christmas from the Emergency Hospital, which was urgently in need of spare cups and saucers as well as odd pieces of linen, old sheeting and cotton material. The material was needed for medical dressings.

Seven milk retailers were before the court just before the holidays. They were charged with adulterating full cream milk by adding skimmed milk. There were six pleas of not guilty. The magistrate mentioned the various tests which had been made on the delivered milk to the dairy and decided that all accused were indeed guilty. He fined each £5 with costs.

Guernsey milk retailers decided to form a protective group, which they hoped would assist them with the many problems they were now facing. Thirty one milk retailers met and all voted in favour of forming an association. At the meeting there were many complaints associated with current deliveries of milk.

An order signed by the chairman of the Prices Determination Board gave the maximum price at which local tobacco could be sold at 2s 11d per ounce and 3s 6d for cigarettes made from the locally-produced tobacco.

About 1,000 schoolchildren were given a special treat at the Regal Cinema just before Christmas in 1943. There were films, displays of dancing and carol singing with Kennedy Bott at the Compton Organ (now in Jersey). At the end of the entertainment, Archie Winterflood, Education Council

66

■ FESTIVE PLEA: Islanders faced another Christmas under German Occupation during December 1943.

Secretary, thanked the Special Aid for staging the event. This was the time of cycle taxing in Guernsey and people with such transport were invited to call at their various parish halls to pay up. The fine for not paying the tax would not exceed £2. Also to be paid at parish halls were the taxes on horses and dogs.

It proved a very quiet time in Sark over the Christmas period. Family parties were the order of the day. In peacetime, the air would have vibrated to the sound of discharging sporting guns when competitions were in progress. Some islanders in Sark had been organising parties of some 30 people in the weeks leading up to the festive season. Each person took food for sharing and stayed the night at the address thus beating the curfew restrictions.

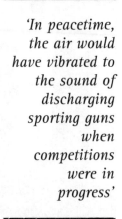

'In peacetime, the air would have vibrated to the sound of discharging sporting guns when competitions were in progress'

There was a moan from a reader of the *Press* that clocks in St Peter Port varied in time. A report stated that it was not thought there was much variation. However, readers were advised to call the telephone exchange if they wished to set their watches correctly. The report recalled the noon and the 9.30pm gun fired from Castle Cornet. This acted as a timekeeper for most of the island.

News was received in Guernsey via a camp for internees in Germany that Bonny Newton had received the DFC for his wartime exploits. After, Christmas dances were being organised at the Lower Central Hall. Billy Shepherd and his Carlton Players dance band provided the music. The advert included in small print and brackets: 'Local people only' – in other words – 'Germans keep out!'

A boxing tournament at the Regal Cinema resulted in the total proceeds of the show – £75 – being given to the St John Ambulance Brigade. Presumably members of the voluntary section of the movement had been on duty at the event to patch up damaged boxers.

The Children's Emergency Bureau was getting very short of stocks for providing clothing for youngsters. Anybody who owned old sheets from which nappies could be made were asked to donate them to this good cause.

So another year of German Occupation came to an end. Stretching ahead was 1944 when the D-Day Invasion would take place. But for the Channel Islanders this would bring no relief.

With the Allied Forces driving through France, contact with the Continent became much worse and supplies of essential commodities dwindled. Eventually people were very grateful for the arrival of the Red Cross ship Vega with food parcels and flour, but it took another 12 months for this relief to reach Jersey, Guernsey and Sark. Liberation would not come until 9 May 1945.

A new year occupied

'THIRTEEN Canadian Airmen Saved off Guernsey' was a headline in the *Guernsey Evening Press* on 3 January 1944. The report stated that on New Year's Eve, 11 Canadian airmen were forced to bale out from their heavily damaged, four engine bomber.

Their plane disappeared into the sea and they landed on a reef of rocks to the north of the island where they were in imminent danger of being drowned. Their yells and rockets were noticed from the shore and they were rescued by members of the German forces, who brought the 11 airmen safely to land.

On the morning of New Year's Day, two further Canadian airmen were picked up from their rubber dinghy off the north coast of Guernsey. They had been forced to bale out from another destroyed aeroplane and were rescued after they had spent the night on the open sea.

The bodies of two other airmen had been washed ashore in Guernsey. They were buried at Fort George but after the war were taken back to America, being members of the United States Air Force. The body of an American sailor, which was washed ashore, was also returned to his own country.

With the start of yet another year of Occupation, it became obvious that newsprint was getting low. The two local newspapers were appearing on alternate days and soon each issue of the *Guernsey Evening Press* consisted of only one sheet, with German and local news sharing the front page. The back page was given over mainly to advertisements and the comment column plus a few news paragraphs. By the end of April, the length of each page was cut by half but there were at least two of these smaller pages.

Reporting on the New Year's Eve celebrations, the *Press* suggested that, as the clock chimed midnight, many war-weary islanders must merely have stirred in their sleep, disinterested in life. Others prodded their small fire to life, raised a glass in farewell to the old and to welcome the new, sighed as they took

LEN DUQUEMIN
Tottenham Hotspur

■ INJURED: A pulled muscle prevented popular Vauxbelets footballer Len Duquemin (pictured here playing for Spurs) from playing for several weeks in 1944.

a new grip on life and braced themselves to meet the future with all that fate held in store for them.

The writer of this report revealed that some 500 young people did dance in the new year – rather a contrast to the thousands who had done so a few years before. The biggest dance was held at the Ladies' College in the Grange and was organised by the Essential Commodities Committee's Sport Club. More than 180 attended this event.

Reports of other dances held on New Year's Eve were printed. Most of the local bands and artists were out and about helping to make the entertainment go with a swing, at a time when the island began to face serious shortages of supplies.

The comment writer tried to be practical by telling the story of a St Peter Port woman who had used her garden wall to grow a fine crop of loganberries. The writer suggested that other house owners might be tempted to do likewise in order to provide jam for their respective families.

The *Press* reported that Len Duquemin, the popular Vauxbelets footballer, who had been noticed limping during the game with Vale Rec, now had to use a walking stick. His right leg, injured above the knee, was swollen and would prevent him from playing for a few weeks. The injury was later diagnosed as a pulled muscle.

A local cyclist was catching the attention of people as he rode up the Grange. He was propelling his machine with his heels claiming that he generated more power using this method.

There was a tragic death in Jersey on Boxing Day. A man who had bent over to couple two railway trucks at Grouville got his head jammed between the buffers. A verdict of accidental death was recorded.

Members of the Island Police Force had just completed the delivery of more than 200 packets of tea from internees in Biberach. The internees had sent the packs for delivery to their relatives in Guernsey.

The *Press* reported that certain people were making a meagre living by delivering brine to householders for the salting of food. Some were delivering tar for mixing with ashes, thus making fairly good fuel.

Police Sergeant Edward Pill thought he heard a pig grunt when he visited a farm on another matter. He was right! The pig was found and the farmer was fined £5 for keeping such an animal for more than six months without registering it with the Farm Produce Board.

A man who entered a building at Fort George without permission died following an explosion as he re-emerged. An inquest heard that the building contained ammunition and was out of bounds to civilians.

The Press Shop was advertising a special show of ladies' 'Parisian' handbags and Sarnia Products was offering Scourex for cleaning pots and pans, baths and sinks for the low price of 10d.

To mark the second anniversary of entertainment at the Lyric Theatre, New Street, St Peter Port (long demolished), there was a specially illustrated souvenir of a forthcoming programme entitled 'Hits – the Best Programmes of 1943, in 1944'. They were great shows, which I never missed.

Deputy's wartime trial should never have been

THE Royal Court was full to capacity on Saturday, 8 January 1944, to hear the former Flour Controller for the Essential Commodities Committee, Deputy F. T. Hill-Cottingham, found guilty of attempting to obtain 56lb of flour from the committee's stores. He was fined £200 plus costs, the alternative being three months in prison.

After the war, he was given a royal pardon following a careful study of the court proceedings. Pleading not guilty to the charge, the former controller maintained that the flour mentioned in the charge was fowl food and simply sweepings from the store. It was unfit for human consumption.

The Bailiff, Victor G. Carey, told the accused that he acted wrongly, even if the flour was unfit for humans. It should have been directed to others who could have made use of it commercially. He had been wrong to take the initiative in such a matter.

This was a message to all in public office in difficult or other times to be ultra careful in their actions. However, having been advised to write to the Home Office, Mr Hill-Cottingham received a full pardon from the King, clearing him of all infamy. He was told by a law expert that the case should never have come to court.

Evidently, in January 1944, the few civilian motorists still on the road – and some cyclists – were disregarding the one-way signs in certain streets. The *GEP* took it upon itself to state that such disregard for traffic signs was 'nothing to be proud of'. It was suggested that to observe one-way signs in future would be a good New Year's resolution. Strange. So far as cyclists are concerned, they still seem oblivious to the signs.

The *GEP* announced on 12 January that there would be pork for all in the coming week. Four ounces, including bone, would be available for each person holding a ration card. It was explained that the Essential Commodities Committee had received half a pig whenever an animal was slaughtered. Initially the meat was issued to butchers, but it was considered that the spread had not been fair. Therefore, the committee put further supplies in cold storage and now had enough for everybody to have a share.

It was reported that during 1943, 23,918 pairs of shoes had been issued through the Controller of Footwear at Ladies' College; a total of 13,500 people who applied had had their requirements satisfied; this averaged 60 satisfied customers a day.

Night prowlers were about in the island, breaking into properties in the hope of obtaining food. A report in the *GEP* recorded that in recent incidents, the telephone had come in handy with householders sending out warnings if they had been the subject of a break-in. In one instance, a telephone bell ringing in one home evidently frightened the prowlers away; they were lead to thinking that an alarm had sounded. In another instance, thieves gained entry to the essential commodities store at St Joseph's School and made off with a quantity of flour.

In this month, news was received of the death of Arthur Winterflood, brother of Archie, the Education Secretary. The

■ HUNGRY YEARS: A St John Ambulance man and German Navy personnel unload Red Cross parcels at the White Rock.

deceased had lived for 20 years in Australia and was serving with the armed forces of that country when he was drowned in action. He had served in the First World War and had been wounded.

The Rev T. Davis (vicar of St James-the-Less now St James Concert Hall) had completed 20 years. Only three vicars at that time had been in office at St James for over 20 years.

One letter-writer complained to the authorities about logs being delivered to homes in a sodden state. The correspondent suggested that after being felled, trees should be kept under cover to dry out.

Rats were becoming a real problem in Guernsey and the authorities decided to take action in a bid to control the pests. People presenting tails to specific addresses would receive one half-mark for every three rats destroyed. The cash would be provided by The Destruction of Rats Committee.

The keeping of goats was growing in popularity and the *Guernsey Press* reported that one family at St Peter's now had four such creatures, which were providing good amounts of milk for family and friends.

Many people will remember PC Hank Reeve. In January 1944, it was reported that he had signed up as a string bass and sousaphone player with Ernie Keyho. Previously, he had been a member of the Lyric Orchestra. I remember him as quite a character with plenty of humour and yarns.

There was good news for some cyclists. A total of 440 such people had been selected to receive tyres for their cycles. The authorities had been careful to issue them to people in need of their machines to get to work each day. Cyclists were warned that one size could no longer be obtained from France.

Cobblers were ordered not to resole shoes if it was thought possible to patch them. Supplies in general were dwindling and things would get worse.

Bailiff Victor G. Carey issued a warning instigated by the Germans about the Fire Brigade having to turn out repeatedly to chimney fires. It was suggested that this was because soot had not been cleaned away – something to which householders should attend.

A welcome winter gift

THE *Evening Press* announced on 21 February 1944 that six of 11 expected cases containing some 120 parcels had arrived in the island from Laufen internment camp.

Postmaster C. H. Chapple said that they would be delivered soon but would have to be signed for. These parcels had been sent from local internees in Germany to relatives and friends in Guernsey and must have been very welcome. The parcels contained, for instance, Christmas cake and puddings, beef rissoles with rice and peas, sliced bacon and sifted sugar.

There was a reminder in the newspaper that the next day would be Shrove Tuesday.

'In spite of the rigours of rationing, many families are planning to have a few pancakes,' reported the paper.

It was with regret that the *Evening Press* reported the death of Arthur Harrison, co-proprietor and editor of the *Jersey Evening Post*. He was 71 and had been associated with the *JEP* for half a century. He was described as having a vivacious and able personality.

Cyclists travelling to work along the coastal road from the north received a soaking on 25 February as waves lashed the sea walls. It was also a very cold day.

There seemed no end to crime in Guernsey. Thieves broke into a bakery in Allez Street, St Peter Port and made off with 140lb of bread loaves and flour. Some of this might have been sold for a high price on the black market, which was never stamped out during the Occupation.

Women were pleased to read that, under a strict rationing process, they could apply for one pair of rayon stockings. The price would be 10s – rather expensive, I would have thought, at that time.

Young women were wanted to form a football team. They were asked to apply to Miss M. Le Gallez, Le Gran Belle, St Andrew's.

A leading store was advertising oat husks for sale. These

would be suitable for fowls or for bedding for rabbits.

Guernsey's theatrical group, the Sarnia Players, had just completed a commendable exchange with a contemporary company in Jersey – the Fifty-Fifty Club. In barter for three plays it had presented in Guernsey, it had secured three from Jersey. These were entitled 'The Hand of the Strangler', 'Busman's Honeymoon' and 'Happy Ending'.

Ninety children (65 between the ages of 10 and 12 and 26 of 12 to 14 years) from both primary and private schools would be sitting the entrance examination the next day (26 February) at the Intermediate School, Burnt Lane, St Peter Port. The candidates would be examined in English, arithmetic and French. It was expected that some 40 of the children would begin their further studies at the school after the Easter vacation.

On 22 February, snow covered the country parishes. At Carmel, St Martin's, a huge snowman had appeared in the garden of a house attracting much attention.

For the second time in the winter of 1944, the Lyric playhouse in New Street was closed for a week because of illness.

The States Rat Destruction Committee said in February that now was the time for islanders to help rid Guernsey of the pests. A spokesman said that once a house got infested with such vermin, it always proved difficult to get rid of them. Inspectors had made 6,026 visits to 1,128 properties in 1943. Some of the rat-infested properties had been called on once a week. Marquand's, the ship chandler, advertised 'breakback' traps for catching both rats and mice.

Materialistic values

ORMER gatherers took advantage of a suitable tide on 1 March 1944 to harvest the shellfish. Catches were reported to be good and the price high. Most of the ormers were sold to the public by the gatherers themselves. These shellfish must have come in very handy to frustrated housewives trying to feed their families each day, especially in that week when the authorities decided that there would be no meat ration.

Rusks sent from France for the benefit of the baby population were causing a problem. The authorities announced that the rusks would break in pieces at the slightest pressure being applied to them. The remnants could not be exchanged for whole ones.

Islanders were being given permission to grow tobacco plants on their outside land but only limited areas could be cultivated with such a crop and the land had to be owned by the planter. All other land had to be used for the cultivation of food producing crops. It was not permissible to raise plants under glass.

Food parcels being sent to Guernsey from internment camps in Germany were not simply a one-way trade. For instance, four chess sets were sent from Guernsey to Laufen and 18 internees in one hut were playing regularly.

An elderly woman signing herself 'Inasmuch' wrote to the *Guernsey Evening Press* suggesting that the age of children due to receive a ration of chocolate should be dropped from 17 to 14. The chocolate saved could go to giving elderly women a treat. She noted that the elderly men got their ration of tobacco but for elderly women there was nothing.

A boy, aged 14, who had been found guilty of stealing in Guernsey, was to be sent to the Boys' Home in Jersey and would remain in detention there until he reached the age of 16.

A farmer who was caught driving a horse and cart in Fountain Street while being drunk was fined £1 or eight days in prison.

It was 18 months hard labour for a man involved in a poison-pen case in Guernsey. The accused had been in prison at the time of the alleged offence and had written two letters from his cell threatening to kill a woman companion if she failed to be loyal to him while he was incarcerated. He told the Royal Court that he had not meant the letters to be found on clothing he sent for washing. Besides the prison sentence, the accused was bound over for three years.

Accidents were becoming numerous and sometimes unusual. At St Peter Port Harbour, a bale of straw being unloaded from a cargo vessel struck a man causing a spinal injury. In another incident, a man sustained burns to his hands while attempting to remove from a house a flaming bucket of tar.

During early March 1944, a resident of Sark was killed by a falling tree. The man sustained a broken back and did not survive his injury. The accident happened when he was engaged in felling the tree.

There was also a fatal accident in Guernsey when a man was struck by a girder being moved by a crane at St Peter Port Harbour. The man sustained multiple injuries. At an inquest, the coroner commented that there had seemed to be some negligence in the handling of the girder.

It was obvious when studying the newspapers of the time that in 1944 stocks of all materials were becoming scarce. The medical officer of health, in an attempt to ease the situation, appealed through the *GEP* to people who might still have sheets and towels, which they could spare for the needy. Such items, it was stated, could not now be acquired through the normal channels.

Miss Aimee Gardner was reported to be making 90 allocations a week to those recipients in the Aged Poor Fund. It meant an expenditure of £23 a week. The fund had been launched in August 1942 to help people in dire financial straits.

Jersey's bailiff was asking islanders to go through their linen cupboards to try and find some article of clothing or old footwear 'to supply the needs of those less fortunate'. The Used-

Up Clothing Department was ready to receive unwanted items.

The *Guernsey Press* reported that the use of tar being used to mix with ashes was on the increase and depots had been opened up where such could be collected. The paper stated that tar used to be employed to paint buildings, such as the black sheds at the White Rock and the railings outside the States Plantations.

Supplies start to run out as others come in from afar

ISLANDERS would have to be on their guard again from 23 March 1944. The *Press* announced that two very well-known police officers would soon be back on duty after both having undergone operations. Police sergeants Robert Kimber and Charlie Le Lievre were now fighting fit.

I remember both and in those days such guardians of the law had a way of getting things settled without much of the red tape and paperwork now demanded. There was one thing about such officers – you did not dare play around with them.

It was with regret that the *Press* announced the death of Mr C. F. Hobbs, for many years the coxswain of the lifeboat, Queen Victoria. His death occurred at the Emergency Hospital after he had experienced a month of illness. He was 60 years old and acknowledged as a very good sailor.

A septuagenarian from the Vale informed the *Press* that the pair of boots he was wearing in March 1944 had been purchased at the Wembley Exhibition before the war and they were still 'going strong'.

A list of depots was being provided for public use from where saltwater would be available. Initially it was available only from Piette.

Twenty tons of seed potatoes had arrived from France. They would be used to meet permits already issued. No further ones would be granted at present.

John Leale, president of the Controlling Committee, placed an appeal for farms to release for general use any spare root crops. He stated that there was a great scarcity of roots available because of the partial failure of the 1943 potato crop.

Candles and nightlights were no longer available in any quantity in Guernsey and the Essential Commodities Committee issued a statement that all permits for these were being withdrawn. Only in very exceptional circumstances would a permit be issued.

82

■ PUTTING UP FIGHTS: The late Steve Picquet was closely involved in boxing tournaments and in March 1944 suffered from gas poisoning.

There must have been plenty of meat on the black market in Jersey at the end of March. Thieves broke into a butcher's store and made off with 200lb worth.

Food of another kind arrived in Guernsey in late March; a total of 2,800 ormers were sent from Sark and were sold in the Fish Market.

From Biberach camp in Germany, eight parcels of cigarettes came into the island for relatives and friends of the internees.

Steve Picquet, the boxing matchmaker, was taken to hospital in late March suffering from gas poisoning. It was thought a gas tap had been inadvertently left on in his home.

People in Sark were shocked to hear that a sporting girl who fractured a leg had now had it amputated. She was described as a swimmer and all-round sportsperson, very prominent on the hockey field.

Easter potato seeds bring ration security hope

ISLANDERS reading the *Guernsey Evening Press* on 5 April 1944 were pleased to hear that their health services officer, Dr A. N. Symons, was back on duty at Hirzel House. Due to blood-pressure problems, he had been away from his medical duties for a considerable time.

There was a mild rush at the St Peter Port Post Office on 12 April to obtain the new 2d blue issue stamps; purchasers were limited to 10 because of paper economy.

The Brock Road Methodist Church schoolroom was packed on Easter Monday when 32 of Miriam Le Page's 40 music pupils provided a concert of 50 items. Proceeds totalling £13 13s 4d went to the St John Ambulance. Miss Le Page received a bouquet of flowers – a gift from her pupils.

A total of 150 tons of seed potatoes arrived from France on 14 April and the Potato Board acted quickly because of the need for immediate planting. On the Saturday morning, growers were able to collect their seed.

Most Town people in need of the potatoes were able to obtain their allocation on the Saturday while country folk, who were late being informed of the seed arrival, formed the bulk of the queue that filled the entrance to Hirzel House when the office opened on the Monday. There appeared to be enough for all permit holders.

The board warned that there would be rigid inspection to see that the areas planted corresponded with the amounts signified on each individual permit. People were warned that the seed was not to be used for any other purpose. If instructions were followed, it was estimated that the potato ration could be maintained into 1945.

It would seem that Guernsey still had its share of vandals way back in 1944. Before the Police Court were four schoolboys; they had broken 24 panes of glass in an unoccupied house in Mount Durand. The Magistrate reprimanded the culprits and

■ TREASURED: A wartime potato store.

ordered their parents to pay damages.

After 60 years of driving, coachman Joseph Gordon of Allez Street was retiring. He was a well-known coachman and had worked for Davey's and Perchard's Stables and driven the Forest, St Martin's and Cobo buses.

A letter writer to the *Guernsey Press* wished to congratulate two islanders whom he considered were providing a good service during very troubled times. One picked out was Mr Ozanne, head gardener at Candie Gardens. He was said to have skilfully preserved the beauty of the gardens with seed saved from locally-grown plants.

How well I remember Mr Ozanne. He was a Methodist local preacher and a very Christian-like man, very much of the old school.

The second man to receive praise was Guernsey's official rat catcher, who was said to be pursuing his work by more scientific methods than those of the Pied Piper of Hamelin Town, with equally remarkable results. The name of this gent was not printed, but the letter writer concluded: 'Well done, Frank, and your grand little terrier'.

Vermin had become a problem in Guernsey and the authorities had made frequent appeals to islanders to do their utmost to help control rats and mice.

Six depots had now been established in the island for the distribution of salt water. It was considered by the authorities that this scheme would be of great benefit to islanders as it would remove the need of having to travel into the original one depot in Town. Because of the scarcity of salt, brine was in great demand for cooking purposes.

On 21 April, the last of the broadsheet newspapers was published by the *Guernsey Evening Press*. From now on, each publication would be of a size more like a tabloid and would replace the one broadsheet, which up to now had been maintained on alternate days with the *Guernsey Star*. Of course, the make-up of the pages remained the same.

A cookery expert advised that Polish potatoes, evidently available in the island, could be cooked complete with skins; they had a distinctive flavour. She also suggested that new potatoes from local crops should be treated in the same way right through the season and certainly until all danger of shortage was over.

Extra potatoes leave housewives chipper

WITH the new format of the *Guernsey Evening Press* introduced on 3 May 1944 came the unexpected news that the Forest Parish Church would be reopened for public worship on Sunday, 7 May. No reason for this decision was given. The church had been closed because of its closeness to the airport and, at this stage in the war, it does not seem to me that the area was any the less dangerous.

On the previous Sunday, the Sunday School anniversary was held at Emmanuel Baptist Church, St Saviour's and some 60 children took part. It was observed that the lack of French in such services was noticeable and went to show that, even at St Saviour's, the rising generation inclined towards English.

Fishmongers were warned that they must see fish cards before selling spider crabs to customers. The amount supplied had not to exceed two-and-a-half pounds per head in a household. Long queues were reported at the Fish Market.

There would be an opportunity for women to cry about their misfortunes into new handkerchiefs: a limited quantity had arrived from France. They had coloured borders and would sell for 1s 6d each plus purchase tax.

Islanders were going to get 'the pip' in May. The jam ration would be marmalade. It would contain pips that could not be extracted from the pulp. The *Guernsey Press* stated that no blame should be attached to the Guernsey Jam Co for these pips in the ration.

There was good news for housewives on 8 May. The authorities announced that there would be an issue of 2lb of new potatoes per head that week. It was hoped that the ration would continue in greater quantity as the season progressed. The *Guernsey Press* observed that this was, for some, a long potato fast, especially for those who did not grow their own crop. There should be no waste from these indoorgrown ones.

Fifty men were required for the spraying of potatoes against an invasion of Colorado beetle. Two inspectors were required, with 10 foremen and 38 to do the spraying. In order to decide on the amount of potatoes needed for islanders until the end of April 1945, householders and growers were ordered to complete forms so that an assessment could be reached. These were published in the *Guernsey Press*.

Percy Dorey of the Glasshouse Utilisation Board informed growers that no permits would be issued for the future growing of chrysanthemums.

The comment section of the *Guernsey Press* released information to the effect that thought was being given to forming what would probably be a residential home for the elderly. They would be able to occupy a room of their own in the home but would be able to mix with others and take part in activities provided in the public rooms. It was stressed that such a scheme would not be in opposition to hotels. It was envisaged that trained staff would be available on the premises.

A few editions later, Marguerite Ross, who was planning to open this new facility, wanted the *Guernsey Press* to explain further that the project she had in mind was an entirely private venture and would not need outside funding. The unit would be for men wishing to give up housekeeping.

A disgusted reader complained about the practice that he had discovered whereby, unless a customer purchased a cabbage, he or she could not also buy either a cauliflower or green peas.

Women rose early to be out at the end of curfew at 6am one May day to queue for sandals. In some instances, they had breakfast standing on the pavement outside shops. Quite a lot of knitting was also done during the three to four hours wait. One old woman of 79 was in one of the queues and the *Guernsey Press* observed that in no way did she complain about the long wait. In fact, she agreed that it was only fair for her to take her turn. There was a complete sellout of the sandals, with some would-be purchasers going home empty-handed.

The grinding mill at Charroterie was working again much to the relief of people who wanted to have their corn turned into a useful commodity.

Children aged 17 and under would be getting a small ration of chocolate cream costing 9d; this would be issued twice in a fortnight.

Eric Snelling, manager of the Regal Cinema, was in need of an upright piano; it had to be in good condition.

Shrapnel injury prompts an air raid warning

A man was injured while walking through the Pont Vaillant Lane during an air raid on 25 May 1944. He was struck by falling shrapnel from a German anti-aircraft shell, attended to by St John Ambulance and taken to hospital with injuries to the stomach, thigh and face. The *Evening Press* suggested that this accident should be a warning to the civilian population to take shelter as soon as firing began.

Men's and boy's two-piece suits had arrived from France and would be available at gents' outfitters. The gentlemen's suits would retail at £8 8s 2d, with the boys' at just over £7. Also available were what was described as 'boys' knickers' – evidently the old-fashioned way of describing underpants. These were made locally in a larger style than previously obtainable and were priced at 16s 3d per pair.

'Cycle thefts were on the increase and the Guernsey Press reminded cyclists of Jack Warner's warning: "Mind your bike!" Things don't seem to have changed'

The Santangelo Orchestra, supported by vocalists, played at Candie Auditorium at Whitsun at 8.15pm; the admission charge was just 7d.

The *Guernsey Press* announced that there was a great deal of work to be done in the island's gardens, especially those at the front of houses. It was suggested that this was rather a pity when the island was so short of food. In some cases, fruit trees had not been pruned. It was revealed that many owners of gardens were employing elderly men, from 65 to 75 years old, who were glad to find occasional work; they were even doing household chores, including mixing tar and coal dust. The wage rate was 6s to 7s a day: seems like slave labour to me – but those were the times.

■ TAKE COVER: A hangar at Guernsey Airport damaged by the RAF during the German Occupation.

The Water Board was getting worried about the supply because of a long, dry spell. It warned the population that all wasteful practices must stop immediately.

I wonder if our German 'visitors' were taking any notice of this advice.

Cycle thefts were on the increase and the *Guernsey Press* reminded cyclists of Jack Warner's warning: 'Mind your bike!'

Things don't seem to have changed.

A sentence of two years hard labour was imposed on three people in Jersey found guilty of stealing pigs.

Some 600 people flocked to the Fish Market on the Saturday before Whitsun. The *Guernsey Press* reckoned that the public had been enchanted by tabulated results published in regard to the average amount of 'meat' to be extracted from a given number of crabs. Most of the small talk in the queues centred on this topic. Further supplies of fish, including a consignment from Sark, were expected on the Saturday afternoon. Should any still be available at the end of the day, the Market would reopen on Whit Monday morning.

The King Edward Sanatorium was in need of a staff nurse, an assistant nurse and a probationer.

The Guernsey Jam Company had tomato puree for sale, but customers had to bring their own bottles and corks; it was selling for 1s a bottle. The drought broke on 30 May when rain finally arrived to revive crops and wash down roads. A couple of days later, temperatures soared and, on arrival at work, one cycle dealer found six with flat tyres stacked against his premises. The excessive heat of the day before had unstuck patches on inner tubes, allowing the air to escape.

It was a difficult job keeping cyclists on the road. In some instances, people resorted to a hosepipe strapped to the wheels. It was possible to cut bad sections out of inner tubes and splice the two cut ends together. But there was a limit as to how many times this could be done. Another problem was securing the right solution to do both the splicing and patching.

The rationing of wood fuel came into operation at that time – only people submitting coupons or permits could be supplied, but this did not apply to kindling wood.

A diabetic man from La Moye, Vale discovered that an intruder had stolen part of his crop of rhubarb and what was left had been damaged. He had grown it because it was one of the few foods he could eat with his condition – of course, without a sugar coating.

The Rev R. Douglas Ord received news of the death of the Rev Dr Frederick Luke Wiseman, the ex-president of the English Methodist Conference. Dr Wiseman was the moving spirit in the compilation of the Methodist Hymn Book published in 1933 and he introduced it to Guernsey on one of his frequent visits. He had been a noted preacher and a composer.

News from second front puts Germans in a spin

ON 7 JUNE 1944, the *Guernsey Evening Press* reported the previous day's landings by Allied troops along the French coast. 'Anglo-American Launch Invasion Attacks in West' read the black headlines.

For the Channel Islanders, it was good news, but until liberation on 9 May 1945, the islands would be almost cut off from the outside world except by air – a risky business.

Neither the Germans nor the civilian leaders in the islands knew if the D-Day invasion would take in the Channel Islands. It was feared that if a landing was attempted, the Germans would strongly resist the Allied forces and many civilians would be killed or wounded. Almost with panic speed, on 7 June the German officer in charge in Jersey slapped an order in local newspapers regarding the curfew time; it was to start at 9pm and end at 6am as normal.

If fighting began, further information would be given through the display of wall placards. In the event of fighting, the blue night permits would lose their validity.

All bays were immediately closed to civilians. All civilian events were closed down, including plays and variety shows. Church concerts were called off and dances cancelled. Guernsey waited, not knowing what to expect – but for the distant rumble of guns in France, all was quiet.

As the Americans pressed on towards St Malo and beyond, the plight of the islands became worse. But as Christmas arrived, the Red Cross ship Vega came on the scene loaded with food parcels and flour and in May 1945 came liberation. But for now, islanders had to tighten their belts and hope and pray for a speedy deliverance.

The paper declared that, the larger the number of food crops grown in Guernsey, the less frequently people would have to pay black market prices. At the end of 1943, the black market price for dried beans ranged from 4s to 5s a pound. Growers were now to be paid a high price by the States for the production of beans so that islanders could buy them at a lower price than the actual cost of production. This was being done as it was expected that January 1945 would be a lean period for food.

The *Press* suggested that if islanders were in their homes, it would be kindly to leave their front doors unlocked so that passers-by might seek shelter should an air raid occur.

A large crowd attended the German military band concert at Candie Gardens on Sunday, 5 June, but on the Monday the ARP announced that there would be no further events there for the present.

As from 6 June, the morning bus service on all routes would cease, Saturdays excepted. With the Anglo-American forces ashore in Normandy, schools in Guernsey were closed and the *Press* advised that it would be wise, at least for now, not to hold religious services. Then came the announcement that bus services on all routes would be suspended until further notice.

Six thousand rations of salted sand eels were being offered for sale in the Fish Market. They would retail at 1s a pound, the ration being a quarter-of-a-pound per head.

The *Press* observed that because of the ban now imposed on large gatherings of people, those organising entertainment had suddenly lost their hobby. However, some of the player groups had decided to keep up rehearsals in the hope that performances could be resumed in the near future. It was observed that the recent ban on entertainment had forced islanders to stay at home. The *Press* pointed out that this was for the safety of civilians and told parents that now that schools had closed, children should be warned of the need to take shelter if they were playing in the streets when air raids occurred.

In Jersey there were similar restrictions with theatres being closed down. Because people were staying at home, libraries were getting busy with more circulation of books and new customers joining.

The Essential Commodities Committee was on the lookout for coppers – no, not policemen, but household coppers used for boiling clothes. No reason was given for this, but it was probably to prepare for more communal soup kitchens if the need arose. As we read on through the newspapers, this may become clear.

93

'Cowards' put supply of food in danger

THE German authorities took the unusual step of using nearly two columns of the *Evening Press* on 21 June 1944 to describe two civilian drivers in their employ as 'cowards'. Headed 'A Warning', the statement was about two islanders employed by the German Army to move foodstuffs from St Peter Port Harbour to specific depots. They had refused to venture down to the White Rock because of the danger of air attacks.

The Germans said they had always considered it a duty to provide the population of occupied territories with food and other necessary items.

This was particularly true of the Channel Islands where it was impossible to produce all the necessary food locally. For four years the German Army had supplied food to the islands and German sailors had risked their lives protecting shipping carrying such goods. It was suggested that, in turn, members of

■ TO BE DESTROYED: Jerbourg monument before demolition.

the local population should do their duty by cooperating with the German Army in delivering goods from the docks. It was claimed the drivers knew that air-raid shelters at the harbour could be used by them as well as by soldiers and that an alarm was always given in time for workers to take shelter.

'Their cowardice is, to say the least, incomprehensible. As, in spite of reiterated orders, they persistently refuse to do their duty, they have been punished,' read the statement.

The Germans warned that if such cowardice continued, the supply of goods to the civilian population could not be guaranteed.

'The islanders will then have these cowards in their midst to thank for the resulting hardship,' concluded the statement.

It was obviously issued in an attempt to halt what was thought might be a growing sense of revolt among civilians employed by the Germans.

Still on food, one reader of the *Evening Press* wished to know how she could make use of a ration of strong smelling fat.

Several rabbits being kept for food were reported to be dying in quick succession. A reader suggested that this could be due to the Scarlet Pimpernel weed, which sometimes was gathered from the fields with the normal rabbit menu.

On 16 June the front page headlines in the *Press* stated that the Normandy battle was drawing to a climax. There had been terrific Anglo-American losses and, off Jersey, a naval battle had occurred and a destroyer had been set on fire. One German vessel was lost. The Germans were continuing to be very worried about the results of the D-Day landings in Normandy. They issued an order warning islanders that loitering on the streets during or after attacks was forbidden. Those offending in this way would be severely punished.

People would also be severely punished for another crime – setting fire to furze. The Germans also appealed to the public to be careful where they threw lit cigarettes or matches during dry spells. Such action could lead to serious outbreaks of fire.

Churches were again holding their Sunday services; in some

instances, evening worship was moved to the afternoon.

The Controller of Footwear, Mr W. D. M. Lovell, warned cobblers that they should make every effort to conserve rubber and leather. If a sole could be patched, rather than completely replaced, this was the decision to make.

The *Press* decided to pay glowing tribute to the St John Ambulance Brigade. Its members had been on duty right through the Occupation. Ambulances were always manned to respond to emergencies and members of the voluntary section had attended football matches and other events. Now, it was stated, ambulance personnel would also be attending church services in case they were needed for first aid purposes.

The Labour Office was appealing for a large number of men to come forward to fell trees and cut them up. The timber was wanted to keep the home fires burning during the winter.

For once, the *Press* carried local news on the front page. The date was 23 June 1944 and the Controlling Committee of the States warned that unless water consumption was reduced by half, drastic steps would have to be taken. If this could not be achieved, then the supply of water for specific purposes could be prohibited. It was noted that the German forces were being included in this warning.

Hauteville House was reported to have sustained slight damage from recent air raids. The damage consisted mainly of broken panes of glass. On 25 June 1944, the Germans destroyed the Doyle Monument at Jerbourg. The next day the *Press* announced the demolition, which was said to be for military reasons. Evidently, the monument was in the firing line of coastal guns.

A man working in a Castel field on 27 June was injured by shrapnel when a mine exploded. It was thought that a dog wandering in a prohibited area had triggered the explosion.

Normandy battle reports had a propaganda slant

ISLANDERS reading the *Guernsey Press* on 2 August 1944 noted, on the front page, a photograph of the French town of Argentan, which was said to have been left in ruins by American terror attacks.

The caption added that, but for a few soldiers in the hospital, there were no German troops in the area. It was claimed that 150 civilians had been killed. This was a normal propaganda report aimed at showing the Allied forces at their worst.

The *Guernsey Press* ran a column on the current ways and means of obtaining black market tobacco. Many men were paying high prices for locally grown in a bid to satisfy their craving. In some instances, growers were charging high prices for the leaf and this amount was increased by the product passing through other hands. It was alleged that some of the so-called tobacco being sold was in fact not pure at all. Difficult days produced bad trading methods.

In the same edition was an advertisement by a shopkeeper at The Bridge, St Sampson's seeking any quantity of local tobacco – obviously for retailing.

A plot of 10 vergées of onions had been established at St Saviour's, one of the largest areas ever to be devoted to this crop.

In Sark, wild blackberries were being harvested, but it was considered that they were not up to the usual standard. The recent dry, sunny weather had probably affected growth.

Rabbits and rats were still creating a problem for farmers in Sark. Bait and traps seemed to hold no fear for the creatures and the correspondent expressed anxiety about what the situation might be like in a year's time.

On 9 August, the front page of the *Guernsey Press* informed readers that St Malo was holding out in fierce fighting. A sketch was printed depicting E-boats attacking Allied warships. Of course, it was the fall of St Malo that cut off all supplies by sea to the Channel Islands.

The late Graham Buckingham, whom the Germans had sentenced to two years for theft from the enemy, had his photograph featured in the paper of the same date. He was being escorted to St Peter Port Harbour for transportation to the Continent when he escaped. The public was warned that concealing Graham would get them into serious trouble.

There was a chance to keep underclothing in the right place about the body. A quantity of elastic had been secured and could be purchased free of coupons at 10d per linear yard.

Raymond Falla wanted to ensure that any gleaning of cereals should be done in an orderly manner. It would be permitted only after owners of crops had removed the cereals and then only after obtaining permission from the farmers.

Readers of the *Guernsey Press* were able to view a picture of the new German Panther tank said to be the best in the world. Some still think that if this had appeared earlier in the conflict, the tremendous task of winning the war might have been even harder.

A patient at Blanchelande Nursing Home wrote to the paper appealing for easy chairs on which patients could recline. It was explained that some would like to sit out on a flat roof to enjoy some fresh air but were prevented from doing so because of a shortage of seating.

The enlarged organ at Bethesda Chapel was officially brought into use in August. The chapel was filled on a Tuesday for the event and it was declared 'a great day'.

The courts at this time were dealing with cases involving the non-delivery by farmers or growers of potatoes to the Essential Commodities Committee and the illegal sale of dairy products to the public. One farmer was fined £76 for disobeying regulations concerning the production of food and its supply.

Bread rations were to be reduced in a bid to conserve what flour was available. Quantities allowed varied according to the work in which consumers were involved.

However, there was to be an increase in the potato ration.

Wheelbarrows and hand carts were urgently wanted by the Labour Office in order that relief work could be carried out in the Vale and St Sampson's parishes.

A paragraph in the *Guernsey Press* of 14 August informed readers that they could view a picture of a German V1 rocket attack on London, taken by an English photographer. This picture would be on view in the Press Shop in Smith Street, St Peter Port. The Germans were still being very defiant.

Tobacco runs out and electricity is cut off

A PRISONER was at large in Guernsey, having escaped from jail during the night of 17/18 September 1944.

The *Press* carried a notice headed 'Wanted', explaining that the 18-year-old local man had been sentenced on 10 September to five year penal servitude and 12 strokes of the cat. Persons with any information should contact the Police Station immediately.

Within a few days he was back in custody having been found standing in Amherst School playground. He gave himself up without a struggle.

The man had been sentenced by the Royal Court for breaking into a private house and robbing and seriously assaulting a woman.

It was announced that the Regal Cinema would be re-opening for the screening of films. Of the 1,200 seats available, 200 would be for the Guernsey public.

The Lyric Cinema, which had been used as a cinema since June, would be closing down in favour of the Regal. Civilians attending film shows would have to pay for entrance in future at the Regal. The prices ranged from 2s 1d down to 10d.

At present, the Compton organ at the Regal could not be played by Kennedy Bott because of the restrictions on the use of electricity.

A housewife was urgently appealing for shoes for her two children.

'They have no shoes whatsoever to wear in the winter and are unable to wear French shoes', she wrote.

Growers were told that they could sell dried beans for 2s 6d per lb. It would be an offence to increase the price beyond this figure.

By order of the German authority, the electricity supply to the island would be shut off from midnight to 5am in future, and from 26 September there would be an additional curfew from 2.15pm to 7pm daily.

Mr C. W. Burch announced that he was opening a shop in Trinity Square. He was a saddler and harness maker and claimed that he had a large stock of harnesses of every description. He had left another firm to start up on his own.

The end of September 1944 was an unhappy time for smokers. The last ration of imported cigarettes and tobacco was announced. From then on, smokers would have to rely on locally-grown tobacco. The *Press* forecast that the price of local leaf would soar! Some people who had grown their own leaf were having it turned into cigarettes at the Guernsey Tobacco Company.

The German authorities were inviting farmers and growers to offer directly to them ripe fruit and vegetables. Apart from this, it was still an offence to sell direct to members of the armed forces. It was now obvious that the enemy was finding it increasingly difficult to meet the demand for food from its military personnel.

An article in the *Press* dealt with the task of organ blowing, which had now become a necessity because of the electricity curfew.

How I remember doing this job for organists wishing to practice. You had to pump for about an hour for which you were paid a small amount. It was necessary to keep one eye on a lead weight, which moved up and down as the organist varied the demand for air.

If the lead rose too high you were in trouble! This movement of the lead indicated that the organ bellows did not have the required amount of air. There was only one thing to do – pump like mad!

Babies bottle teats were getting extremely rare in Guernsey. At auction sales a teat was fetching over £3.

However, things were able to change!

The States Supervisor, Harry Marquand, decided to impose a price control on teats sold at auction. From then on these teats could not be sold for more than 90 per cent of the cost price. They could now be sold for only a few shillings and none were being offered in auction. The headline on this story read: 'Silencers cheaper.'

The authorities warned that the St John Ambulance service was being restricted because of the lack of petrol. A horse-drawn ambulance was soon to be introduced, but this vehicle would not be able to cover large areas. The motor ambulances would, on non-emergency cases, have to carry more than one patient at a time from country areas. The time had come, it was stated, when the public had to comply with the directions given by the ambulance officials.

Housewives, who were now finding it difficult to cook meals, were being advised to try the sawdust box. This was a biscuit tin, filled with sawdust. The *Press* gave detailed instructions on how to operate such a unit. It was very slow burning and proved reasonably successful if instructions were followed. However, one woman is said to have pressed the sawdust down so firmly that it smouldered for three days, belched out volumes of smoke – and cooked nothing!

Churchill relents on supplies

THE Germans decided in October 1944 to reveal certain information to the public regarding the present shortage of essential supplies in Guernsey. They explained that the invasion of France by Allied Forces had cut off supplies to the island. In view of the possibility of a state of siege, agriculture and industry had been adapted as far as feasible to make the fortress self-supporting.

However, as this could not be sustained over a long period of time, the Commander of the Channel Islands had contacted the German government and had informed its members of the situation. The German government had since indicated its intention of taking the necessary steps in this matter with the Protecting Powers.

Therefore, the local Commander had sent a list of the monthly requirements necessary. The Germans added that any action that the Protecting Powers might take was beyond the Control of the Occupying Forces.

This passing the buck to the Protecting Powers did not go down well with the Bailiff or his colleagues, who responded by letter, pointing out that it had been assumed that the Occupying Powers were concerned for both Army personnel and the civilian population.

Actually Churchill had been against arranging any supplies to be sent to the islands, believing that this would prolong the occupation. However, he finally relented and arrangements were made for Red Cross food and medical supplies to sent.

The House of Travers at the top of Smith Street was celebrating 60 years of business service to the public.

James Jacob Travers had thrown open the doors of the Prince of Wales bar, later to become a hotel. In those 60 years, three generations of the family had managed the business. This was claimed to be the longest established family business in Guernsey.

In 1897, the restaurant was started with a full-scale dinner costing 1s.

Thefts from properties were now rampant. In one instance large quantities of grapes had been stolen from a vinery. Some parts of the vine were completely stripped of fruit. There were also several instances of rabbits being stolen from their hutches.

From the States Labour Office came the sad news that stocks of cycle tyres and tubes had now become exhausted. No further applications could be accepted.

Due to lack of light, the well-known barber in the Canichers announced that he could only cut hair between 9am and 5pm.

Chief Pleas received a report from the North Cinema regarding the lighting of the building when patrons were entering at 7pm. It was not possible to have light because of the restrictions. A panic might be caused if anything untoward happened. It was agreed that the matter should be investigated.

A delicate boy attending the Intermediate School was in need of a wheel to complete his cycle. Readers were asked to assist the lad if they had a wheel of the required size.

Because of the electricity restrictions, the *Press* was finding it difficult to print news and advertisements at an early date. Such items would have to be taken in rotation.

In Jersey certain persons had attempted to escape from the island by boat. They had to be rescued by the German Forces when they ran into difficulties. There was a strong warning of the likely consequences if further attempts to leave the island were detected.

In the edition of the *Press* on 9 October 1944, the death was reported of Captain E. Cowley MBE. He was the Commandant of the Special Constabulary and was just 74. He had been in business in Guernsey for many years and also a recruiting officer for the island during the First World War. Many thousands of men passed through his hands into the British Army. He had gone into business as a tobacconist at No 1, Mill Street, St Peter Port and had remained there for the rest of his life.

According to the *Press*, many islanders were appreciating the small panes of glass, which were replacing large plate glass ones in part of St Peter Port. They helped to add charm to the Town and would be a tourist attraction.

Many shop fronts sported small panes of glass after the Allied Air Force dropped blast bombs in the Old Harbour in an attempt to damage a submarine which was not there at the time of the attack.

I myself was cycling along the Quay at 8.30am on the morning of the attack and took shelter in a small petrol department near the States Office. Afterwards, I was forced to carry my bike up the Pollet, which was littered with broken glass from the shop windows. The Town Church suffered bomb blast with windows damaged. It was lucky that all the bombs fell in the Old Harbour at high tide. Damage would have been far greater if the bombs had struck the quays.

Worker ends up in oven

THE *Press* of 13 October 1944 reported an unusual accident at the Rockmount Hotel, Cobo, the previous day.

Workmen had been constructing an oven to be used for communal cooking at the hotel. One of the men crawled inside the oven to remove residue materials when part of the construction collapsed covering the worker with debris. His fellow workers spent 10 minutes rescuing the poor chap from the oven. It was thought his injuries might include internal damage so St John Ambulance hurried him to hospital.

The States, with German permission, intended to introduce legislation, which would result in confiscation of tobacco leaves and machinery used in the tobacco process should a person be found guilty of other tobacco offences. With the end to cigarette and tobacco rationing, everybody who smoked was relying on locally-grown leaves and this had resulted in black market trading and other offences.

Because of the restriction on power, the Guernsey Tobacco Company announced on 18 October 1944 that it could not accept orders for tobacco leaf cutting or the making of cigarettes until 1 November – another blow to smokers!

One of Guernsey's most familiar figures, Bill Prout, was dead, it was announced in the *Press* on 23 October 1944. It was recalled that Bill used to be heard calling: 'Nice mackerel for sale,' as he hawked his fish cart, not so long ago. He used to sell the fish for four a shilling! Bill had gone to see a doctor and within an hour of leaving the surgery he had passed away at the age of just 59.

Nurses were urgently needed at the Town Hospital. Previous experience was not necessary.

In Jersey, old motor tyres were being collected to provide repair materials for boots and shoes.

The Guernsey Essential Commodities Committee needed large frying pans for the cooking and feeding centres being established.

A number of domestic properties were being sold in Guernsey at this time. Perhaps speculators realised that the war was drawing to a close and housing would be a safe investment in the future. If islanders did purchase for this reason, they would have made very nice profits in the years ahead.

Peter Campbell was presenting 'Keep it Dark!', the show without lights at the Little Theatre. This entertainment was on the Thursday and Saturday at 2.30pm. This was one way of beating the electricity and gas curfew.

There was very sad news from Sark. A five-year-old girl accidentally entered a mined area and caught the full blast of an exploding mine. She died instantly, her brother being seriously injured.

In Guernsey, a young lad had also died having been involved in a box cart accident.

Growers were warned that in future they could not use water for their crops from the mains supply except on Mondays and Thursdays. After watering, all taps and valves had to be properly shut down.

The States accounts showed that the cost for the year in running the Isolation Hospital was £3,465 16s 7d.

It was decided by the German authorities to open additional offices in a bid to speed up the dealing with punishable acts. Directions were given using the military road signing – for instance Red 3 or Yellow 10. This was how the troops found their way round the island.

The first of the Christmas advertising campaign by the commercial world, appeared on 30 October. Millview Café at St Martin's was announcing an Christmas showroom, with books, toys, calendars etc. Almost as early as now!

A sure sign that Christmas was approaching came with the announcement that on 1 November an augmented choir would be a giving a sacred concert at Brock Road Methodist Church, including excerpts from The Messiah.

Operations limited as catgut runs out

AN ATTEMPT by a group of Jerseymen to escape from that island during late October 1944 had been foiled. German troops opened fire on the group, one being killed and the others arrested.

The German report explained that a patrol on the eastern part of Jersey noticed at about 5am, a dark moving object on the beach. A flare was released and four or five people were seen to be busy about a boat. The group took cover, and as they did not respond to a challenge, the Germans opened fire. A civilian was killed and three others taken into custody. The men had been attempting to escape from Jersey.

Concluding the story, the Germans warned that people going on the beach after dark were playing with their lives and could be shot at without warning.

The Guernsey States Public Works Department were erecting four pairs of bath cookers at the upper end of the Fish Market for communal cooking, should this be necessary.

Another pair of containers was being built for the cleaning of vegetables. Wood fuel would be used to heat the necessary water.

The German Commandant issued an order in the *Press* on 6 November 1944 warning people of the need to safeguard food supplies. The legislation covered black market activities and failure to comply could result in jail or, in serious cases, the death sentence.

Guernsey hospitals were running into trouble because of shortages. At the Emergency Hospital only essential operations could be performed. This was because there was a shortage of catgut.

The Germans ordered that the use of all electric cookers had to stop. But owners of such cookers could obtain ration coupons for the purchase of wood fuel.

Growers were warned that the sale of root crops to the German paymaster and to Messrs Timmer Ltd would be prohibited.

The Sarnia Football Council held a meeting and decided that, because of existing circumstances, it was impossible to proceed with the arranged list of fixtures for the season. All future matches would be cancelled.

Bailiff Victor G. Carey announced that the Germans had allowed him to send a radio message to the International Red Cross at Geneva stating the present serious shortage of many essentials in the island and asking for an immediate visit of a Red Cross representative.

Thieves in Sark were having rich pickings. A crock of cream had been stolen, trees cut down at dead of night and removed, poultry taken and larders relieved of meagre rations. It was hoped that the thieves would be brought to book.

Islanders were receiving another form, different to the initial one, in relation to possible communal feeding on a grand scale. It was suggested that since the initial census in August, the situation had deteriorated and the numbers of people expected to use the facility on offer must have increased.

The Guernsey Gas Company warned consumers they must stick to their ration. If they failed to do so, their supply would be cut off and not restored until the company could obtain fresh supplies of coal.

The Lyric Cinema was re-opening for the screening of German films. Thirty seats would be reserved for civilians.

The *Press* carried a reader's letter, which referred to the shortage of matches in the island. The writer recalled a lecture in Guernsey by 1928 by a Red Indian Chief. At that event the chief used a stick and a plank of wood to eventually start a flame. It was suggested by the writer that some firm in the island might provide the necessary equipment for starting such fire should all matches disappear.

A foreign worker had strayed into a German minefield in November 1944 and had caused an explosion. He sustained serious shrapnel wounds and was taken to hospital by St John Ambulance.

Thieves entered H. H. Plummer's bakehouse in Allez Street and made off with 350lbs of flour and 95lbs of bread. Efforts to gain an entry was made firstly with a drill but when this failed, glass window panes were smashed. The alarm was raised by Mr Chapman, who worked at the bakery.

A shop in the Pollet had also been ransacked and money and tinned goods stolen.

Essential supplies dwindle as Islanders wait for Red Cross

AN APPEAL went out from the *Press* on 17 November 1944 requesting people with vegetable root stocks already in their possession not to purchase any further quantities at this stage. This would allow the poorer islanders to secure food for their families.

The Guernsey Gas Company was forced to ration tar to households, including producers of sugar beet syrup and salt. Only one gallon a month would be available per applicant.

Tribute was being paid to the Guernsey Tobacco Company who had supplied 50 million cigarettes and two-and-a-quarter million ounces of tobacco to islanders over the past four-and-a-quarter years. As already reported in this series, the company had at last run out of rationed tobacco secured from France. Only local leaf was now available.

Schools had to contend with intruders during the Occupation. Les Capelles School was broken into and 12lb of biscuits stolen. The biscuits were intended for the pupils.

The German Commandant issued a notice on 24 November 1944 that in future all owners and occupiers of glasshouses watered via the States Water Board were no longer permitted to draw any such water from this source. Those growers who did would be punished.

Bailiff Victor G. Carey, stating that after discussion with the German Commandant, he had received an assurance that the demand for potatoes from the German Forces would not exceed 500 tons including those taken from 1 November.

'Although this is a relatively small proportion of the total season's crop, it represents approximately the stocks of potatoes which we had in our depots,' wrote the Bailiff.

He went on to state that each producer would be allowed to retain 90lb of potatoes for him and his family.

'I know that this entails a great sacrifice, but remember it is a matter of life and death for those without potatoes. I beg all holders of potato ration cards, who have potatoes, to stop drawing rations', concluded the Bailiff.

Arthur Selous was quietly painting his way through the Occupation. One of his oils depicting the Dog and Lion Rock was on view at the Singer Sewing Machine Shop in Smith Street, St Peter Port. He worked as a cycle mechanic in Bill Green's repair shop opposite Singer's premises.

Men forced their way into a pigsty in Mount Row intent on stealing a large sow. They caught the animal a glancing blow with a crowbar but fled without it because of the great noise it was making. They had brought a sack to contain the creature, but it was left behind at the scene. Later, the sow had to be put down by an authorised slaughterer.

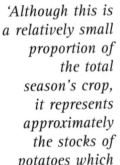

'Although this is a relatively small proportion of the total season's crop, it represents approximately the stocks of potatoes which we had in our depots'

As from 1 December, the working hours for men in the States employ would be from 9.30am to noon and from 2-5pm. Growers and other employers were asked by the States to adopt these hours.

Although shopping hours were listed, with a closing time of 4.15pm, general agreement between traders could not be reached. The authorities said they had no objections to earlier closing than listed, if so desired.

Because of the lack of electricity, Wallace – hairdressers – announced that they could no longer fulfil appointments taken. Customers were asked to contact the firm regarding other work, which they could continue to complete.

Allez Street Bakery warned that no further grinding of sugar beet, carrots and parsnips could take place. However, customers could prepare these products themselves, and the bakery would do the baking and the drying.

In the Comment column of 27 November, the *Press* expressed relief regarding the promise that essential supplies would be arriving in the Channel Islands. These were the medical supplies, Red Cross parcels and flour. But it would be another month before such goods could be distributed to the population. Meanwhile, both civilians, and in fact Germans, struggled on the best they could.

Hungry Islanders resort to theft

IT SEEMED a great shame that with liberation months away, people in Jersey were dying in a bid to escape from their German occupied island.

One man had been shot on a beach while making a bid for freedom, and on 2 December the *Press* reported that four people had been drowned when the boat they were using to try and reach the French coast, had been dashed against rocks.

The German Military Court had pronounced sentences of six to 10 months on six people who had attempted to leave the island. In two cases of rendering assistance to others in a bid to escape, four to six months jail sentences had been given. In four other attempted escapes, sentences of five to 15 months were ordered.

Of course, people did not realise that freedom was approaching, and with the Americans moving right down the French coast, it was a great temptation to try and reach the European mainland.

There was a mean theft at the Town Hospital. Sugar, flour and cooking fat had been stolen. The thief gained access to the hospital by a ladder.

The electricity supply to homes was now to be cut daily at 10.30pm instead of 11pm.

Owing to the seasonal reduction in production, the daily ration of separated milk was likely to fall to half a pint during the next 10 to 12 weeks.

People needing brandy for medical purposes were informed by the Medical Services Officer that all such stocks had now been exhausted.

At Victoria Road Methodist schoolroom, the St John Ambulance members met to form a Relief Association. The main aim was to supply clothing and bedclothes to needy members of the population.

More bread was being stolen, this time from the Town Mills Bakery. It was reported that thieves had made off with 60lbs of bread.

The St John Ambulance had taken delivery of a second horse-drawn ambulance. This one was lighter to pull than the first model. The brigade was still appealing for rubber hotwater bottles and other equipment.

Householders having to use paraffin lamps were advised that by adding a drop of salt water or vinegar to the fuel it would stop smoke developing.

Farmers were told that a limited amount of carbide was presently available to help them light their stables.

Mann's, the Pollet hairdressers, were closing down because of no electricity supply. Customers were invited to arrange for a shampoo and set to be performed at their own homes.

Break-ins were becoming so serious that shopkeepers in Town were employing night watchmen to stand guard. Arrangements were made so that, if these watchmen heard suspicious noises outside the premises, they simply had to lift the telephone receiver without saying a word. The night operator would then inform the police that something suspicious seemed to be happening at a given address.

At Bragg's flour store, Glategny Esplanade members of the St John Ambulance guard team used to secure old tins to cord, criss-crossing them across the approach yard to the store. This certainly was a good alarm system!

The Reverend William Kilshaw, who served as a deputy, wrote to the *Press* beseeching employers not to reduce the wages of men in their employ because they were working shorter hours. He wanted legislation introduced to prevent this and to avoid untold suffering.

The States Telephone Department was appealing to islanders not to use the telephones between 10pm and 6am unless it was vitally important.

Visiting hours at the Emergency Hospital were being reduced because of the present critical situation in the island. At least the patients would have more rest, and not be plagued by endless questions as to their condition!

Joy at news of the good ship Vega

ON THE last days of December 1944, the *Press* concentrated on the arrival of the good ship Vega. She was to sail from Lisbon with much needed supplies for the Guernsey Bailiwick and Jersey, and her arrival was awaited with eager anticipation.

It was on 8 December that the *Press* broke the news of the departure of the Red Cross vessel from Lisbon. Aboard was 750 tons of store. In due course, islanders would be informed as to the method of distribution of the food parcels known to be aboard.

Meetings were immediately held in Guernsey of Red Cross and St John Ambulance personnel.

People with relatives in deportation camps in Germany were advised that there would be a chance of sending letters to the camps by putting them aboard the Vega when she returned to Portugal.

However, it seemed that the initial announcement of the ship's departure was rather premature, to say the least!

On 20 December the *Press* announced that the Vega would be leaving Lisbon that day and was expected to arrive in Guernsey on Christmas Day. Because of the expected arrival of the Vega, the States meeting convened for 27 December was changed to 3 January 1945.

It was agreed that church services take the form of thanksgiving meetings and that collections taken should go to the Red Cross organisation.

By 29 December 1944, the joyful news of the arrival of the Vega hit the pages of the *Press*. The ship glided into St Peter Port Harbour on 27 December – a little behind schedule, but very, very welcome. Hundreds of people had turned out to see the Vega glide to her London berth from where she was discharged of her valuable cargo.

The German train was loaded with the precious supplies with the parcels being taken to St George's Hall and the flour to Bragg's store at Glategny Esplanade. Some sacks of flour were taken to St George's Hall where German troops emptied them to ensure that there were no firearms hidden in the sacks.

St John members kept a nightly vigil throughout the period to ensure that break-ins did not occur. With no electricity they were forced to use candlelight.

By 31 December, the food parcels were ready for distribution. We in the St John Ambulance acted as escorts for the horse-drawn vans, which conveyed the food to depots throughout the island.

Sometimes deliveries made were short in number and I can remember pushing a sack truck loaded with parcels from St George's Hall, up the Blue Mountains to a shop in Town to make good the deficit.

It was all very exciting with much wanted food well wrapped and preserved. For invalids there were specially-prepared packages, and of course, the flour was greatly appreciated by the bakers.

There seemed enough food to go round, and there was also the assurance that the Vega would be returning with further supplies – a promise that was kept.

In recent years, a high-ranking British officer who was in charge of the operation at Liberation to clear German barracks, told me that traces of Red Cross parcels had been located in such areas. To what extent the Germans benefited from Red Cross food is now known, but I reckon there were only isolated cases.

With communal feeding becoming available and so many articles of modern living exhausted, islanders made what they could of the new food from the International Red Cross. They would look forward to further trips of the Vega and be thankful for the great effort made to relieve their misery.

Although they were not aware how long their uninvited 'visitors' would be staying, they were hopeful that 1945 must bring the freedom for which they had yearned for so long.

Well, there were still four months and a few days to go before British troops would march up the White Rock. Those few months of 1945 continued to be tough, but with the Vega busy about her Red Cross work, there was much more hope of survival in the minds of Channel Islanders.

Food arrives but hardships continue

GUERNSEY folk who had been held down for almost five years through German Occupation celebrated the New Year with greater zest than usual. The Allies were winning the war against Hitler and there seemed every chance that the Channel Islands would be liberated during 1945.

But it was not until 9 May that year that freedom came. Before that, the problems in the islands continued. Red Cross food had arrived, but this too had caused problems. The Bailiff was not happy about the contribution islanders were making to help repay the cost of the food being brought in by the Vega. There was also questions about why some of these supplies were being regulated through rationing.

A double brutal murder was reported, which shocked islanders. Communal feeding centres closed down due to a lack of vegetables, and there were meagre supplies of gas and electricity.

In Germany, deportees from the islands were also awaiting liberation from the advancing Allied Forces. Everybody hoped that freedom for those in the islands and in Germany could be achieved safely, and it was!

The *Guernsey Press* of 3 January 1945 was full of news about the arrival of the Red Cross parcels from Portugal. A reporter went to St George's Hall where parcels were being stored and reported 'perfect organisation and willing co-operation' in getting the foodstuff distributed.

'The scene at St George's Hall was impressive in the methodical work in which all was carried out,' observed the reporter.

This consignment of food consisted of 2,650 cases each containing 16 parcels coming from the Canadian and New Zealand Red Cross. This made up a total of 42,400 parcels. Salt, soap and flour had also arrived – all this, for many, just in time!

'For the remainder of their lives the 23,000 men, women and children now in Guernsey will remember the last day of 1944.

■ PRECIOUS FOOD: Islanders collected their Red Cross parcels from shops using prams for the purpose.

They will think of it as Red Cross Parcels Sunday,' wrote the reporter.

For me, as a St John Ambulance cadet, it was a joy to be helping with the handling of these supplies, albeit in a small way.

It was now anticipated that parcels could in future be issued about once a month as the Vega would be making further voyages to the islands. People were advised to always keep some of the food in reserve. There were also instructions on how to use tinned food – a product in very short supply over the past years.

An official notice stated that there would be a possibility of the evacuation in the Vega of islanders needing specialist operations or other medical treatment.

The St John Ambulance reported that all charcoal for use in operating ambulances was exhausted. The Brigade was now restricted to 15 gallons of petrol a week and it was not possible to find additional horses for horse-drawn ambulances. The time had come when some of the work would have to be refused.

Some mothers expecting babies were being thoughtless and selfish by not warning the brigade of their impending need earlier so that cases could be combined.

The *Guernsey Press* could no longer sell newspapers on the street. Only direct orders to homes could be accomplished, and even then this might not always be possible. Readers were asked to share copies if necessary. The *Star* was again publishing on days when the *GEP* did not.

Two promotions were made in the Island Police Force. Constables Frank Le Cocq and Reg Marsh were made up from the rank of constable to corporal – yes, there were corporals in those days.

The two men rose to inspector rank and were very well known in the island after the war. Mr Le Cocq, on retirement from the Police Force, became HM Sheriff and Governor of the Prison.

A States meeting was informed that Red Cross meetings had been held in the island between Red Cross representatives, the

■ THE RED CROSS SHIP 'VEGA' LEAVING ST PETER PORT HARBOUR FOR JERSEY: A lighty-armed German launch saw her clear the Island.

civilian leaders and the German authorities. It had been revealed that the Vega would continue to travel between Portugal and the islands with food supplies. Flour and food parcels should be the priority, therefore other essentials could not be provided in large quantities. It had been a request of the Red Cross that a reserve of food parcels should be created in the islands.

The St John Ambulance Relief Organisation was appealing for help. Overcoats, blankets and mattresses were urgently required as well as donations and help from women in re-modelling garments provided by donors. This organisation had been formed to help the very needy in times of great stress.

Pilfering continues but the property market looks up

THREE cases of pilfering of Red Cross supplies from St George's Hall had been reported to the police. It was stated on 22 January 1945 that the police had investigated three such incidents but quantities of supplies taken were small.

Inspector Albert Lamy revealed that he had put forward proposals to the Essential Commodities Committee to ensure complete safety of the stock.

Only a small quantity of tobacco and soap had been reported missing and two parcels of food were believed to have been tampered with.

In view of the very serious shortage of food in Guernsey, the German authorities issued a notice forbidding stock piling. Any surplus food should be given to less fortunate persons or to the soup kitchens.

The States Controlling Committee also published an order regarding the use of communal feeding and cooking. For instance, people taking food for cooking to bakers had to be properly registered with that bakery. The same applied to feeding centres.

There was not enough Red Cross soap to go round so the States issued a notice that islanders who did not receive a cake of soap in their Red Cross parcels could apply for same in writing, not later than 13 January 1945.

All accumulators not in use on vehicles were ordered to be handed in to the Civil Transport depot.

Several young people were required to train as teachers for the increasing number of children of school age.

The *Guernsey Star* on 10 January made an appearance again, following its closure by the Germans to try and save newsprint. It had been the first interruption in publishing since 29 June 1813 when it was founded.

The Island Police Force was being divided into three sections – Town, North and South – with a station in each. Islanders

123

were asked to use their respective stations to help make the new system work.

A sad story was carried about a man who, having received his first Red Cross parcel, immediately lost it when his bungalow caught fire.

In a bid to curb crime, which was said to be rife throughout the island, the police had recruited more officers who would be

■ FLOUR ARRIVAL: Sacks of Red Cross flour arriving by train at Bragg's Store, Glategny Esplanade.

engaged in their duties from mid-January.

People who had stored lubricating oil in excess of one litre were ordered to hand it in to the States.

The *Star* of 20 January 1945 reported that the property market in Guernsey was booming. Sales of large and small houses and estates continued to attract numbers of investors who were willing to pay considerable sums for properties suitable for their own needs or an investment for the future.

Two islanders were sentenced each to nine months hard labour for cattle stealing. They had appeared before the Royal

■ FREE HANDOUT: Issuing Red Cross Parcels at a grocery store.

Court.

The growing of flowers in glasshouses or on outside land was banned during 1945. In relation to outside land, cultivation might be permitted but not without permission from the States.

There would be a meat ration for 25 January, but the *Star* warned that it would be 'rather smaller than usual.'

A man who sold a packet of tea, which he had received in his Red Cross parcel, was fined £10 or one month in prison when he appeared before the Magistrate's Court. It was considered a despicable thing to do and the defendant ran the risk of losing future Red Cross supplies.

John Leale, president of the Controlling Committee, issued a 'last warning' to milk producers. They had to send as much milk as possible to the Dairy, only keeping back the amount stated in the law. If they failed to respond to this order they could face severe penalties.

The German Commandant told farmers that they were responsible for the safety of their food stocks, especially seed potatoes. Such food should be securely locked away near the farmhouse and barns some distance from their homes should be emptied of all stock. If necessary, food should be stored in more secure locations on neighbouring farms.

Farmers were also being ordered by the Germans to send cattle to the slaughterhouse. Visits would be paid to farms to ensure that this order was being obeyed.

The Guernsey Tobacco Company reported that thieves had stolen a large quantity of cigarettes and pipe tobacco from its factory in Cornet Street. It belonged to customers who had taken it there for the necessary preparation.

Two boys aged 10 and 12 were before the court for breaking into a house and stealing foodstuffs. Their punishment – eight strokes of the birch.

Waiting for the return of the Vega

NO NEWS had been received in Guernsey by the end of January 1945 regarding the Vega's return visit with essential supplies. The Germans had sent several radio messages inquiring as to the ship's movements, but there had been no response.

Therefore, the Bailiffs of Guernsey and Jersey prepared an appeal to the Secretary General of the International Red Cross at Geneva. This message stated that stocks of flour and grain would be exhausted by about 10 February.

'We urgently appeal for dispatch of flour or grain for Jersey and flour for Guernsey, since in the latter island, grinding can only be done by electricity of which no supply is available for this purpose due to shortage of diesel oil and coal,' ended the message.

Soon after the above text was sent, the Vega arrived at St Peter Port on 7 February. The ship carried food parcels, invalid food parcels, soap, medical supplies, salt, tobacco and cigarettes, etc.

There was no mention of flour so the newspapers pressed the authorities for a statement. It came in the *Star* on 10 February.

This was from the Bailiff who said he deeply regretted to inform islanders that the supply of flour would be exhausted in three days after the nest bread ration.

Red Cross parcels would be distributed on 15 February 1945 and again on 1 March 1945. It was hoped to issue increased rations as far as resources allowed on 18 February. Further details were released as to the small increases of rations, which would be issued while Guernsey had no bread.

With all this information came the warning that householders should guard food in their homes because of the great increase in break-ins. Growers packing sheds were also a target for the thieves, several having been ransacked.

All communal feeding centres were to close as from 3 March due to the exhaustion of stocks of potatoes. This was a blow to those who were dependent on these centres.

The Germans, on 28 February, issued a notice in German and English. It informed the troops and civilians that Ernst Lickfeld, a German soldier, had escaped from prison on the island, having been condemned to death. He was now living in hiding and people were warned not to assist him in any way.

It was on 23 February that the *Press* announced that Mr and Mrs J. A. Sigwart of 1, Rockville, Hauteville had been found dead in their home. Mr Sigwart was a retired jeweller. At the inquest reported on 28 February, it was revealed that the couple

■ FOOD AHOY: The hold of the 'Vega' stacked with Red Cross parcels.

had been found dead when police broke into the house.

A witness had seen a bicycle inside the gate of the house and there was a light in the hall. At a resumed inquest, it was decided that Mr Sigwart had developed a brain storm and murdered his wife, and then committed suicide by drowning himself in a bath. A very sad case, which stunned islanders.

Victor Creasey, Electricity Controller, was forced to announce that from Sunday, 25 February, at 10pm all electricity supplies for the general public would be cut off until further notice. This was to ensure a supply to the essential services.

The Germans decided that the welfare of the community no longer permitted well-to-do members of the community to hoard supplies of soap, wine and spirits exceeding their actual needs. All such items, in excess of what was personally needed, would be confiscated and given to hospitals and institutions.

Green's, the cycle people, were appealing for tent canvas for tyre repairing. This service had been offered throughout the long years of Occupation but now Cyril Renouf, the boot repairer who did the stitching, was running out of materials.

It was not only locals who bought these repaired outer covers but also foreign workers who were recent visits to the shop and

■ ABANDONED PILLS: The late Reg Blanchford, Chief Officer of the Transport sector of St John ambulance, collecting drugs from deserted houses.

always seemed to have cash to buy such items, even reconditioned bicycles!

The St John Ambulance Relief Organisation was now

appealing for clothing of all types that would fit schoolchildren.

There were some serious accidents during the Occupation caused in the main by people having to improvise. In one instance in February 1945, a man set himself alight while involved with petrol and a lamp. He later died from his burns. In those days, there was no opportunity to be flown to the UK to a burns unit.

Vale man dies after entering minefield

A 41-year-old man from the Vale, who started to walk through a minefield at La Miellette, Vale, was fatally injured by an explosion.

The deceased and his brother had climbed over a wire fence into the mined area. The brother had been told there were no mines where they were walking and had used this route to get to the beach several times before. They were seeking ormers.

Following the explosion, the 41 year old shouted to his brother that he was seriously hurt. One of his legs was amputated; the injured man died later from shock.

Some of the medical supplies, which arrived on the Vega, could be sold by chemists – Bile beans, Maclean's stomach powder, etc. But it had been discovered that some customers were purchasing more than their fair share. Therefore, in February 1945, the sale of such products was withdrawn while the authorities decided how the situation could be controlled.

Breadless meals were suggested by the *Press*. Sliced cold potatoes was one suggestion, served with butter, jam or cheese.

It was decided that, like ship-wrecked mariners, islanders would be forced to eat very small meals, putting on the table all that could be consumed at that session. People would not feel satisfied, but at the next meal, they would not feel completely famished. The States cookery expert stated that the Red Cross parcels were giving people more concentrated nourishment than they had received for many a day.

Thieves broke into a house at Les Fauconnaires in broad daylight, consumed a pudding on the spot and then removed practically an entire stock of potatoes and vegetables. The house owner was meanwhile working in a nearby glasshouse.

In another instance, thieves who entered a farmer's house in the Castel removed a piece of pork from a rack. In doing so, they spilled a jar of salt but had the kindness to sweep the contents into a corner of the kitchen. It was surprising that they left the salt!

■ DANGER SIGNS: Warnings of minefields were erected by the Germens but sometimes ignored by civilians with disastrous consequences.

Percy Dorey, president of the Glasshouse Utilisation Board, issued a notice to growers of potatoes. It stated that the Germans were insisting that spuds for the troops should be planted immediately. All growers involved were ordered to report the completion of seed to the German authorities either in writing or verbally.

Thieves were now most earnest in their endeavours to secure food. In two instances, householders had received letters informing them to report at an address at a specific time. On returning home, they found that their houses had been entered and food stolen – in one instance a Red Cross parcel.

Children's clothing, toys and nursery furniture was being

sought by the Hospital Board. It was proposed to open a new home for children.

Nothing seemed safe in Guernsey in February 1945. Even telephone poles were being attacked.

A man was given a two-week jail sentence and ordered to pay £10 damages. Two other poles in the district had also been felled, but no evidence was offered on these. So long as this man had fuel for his fire, he did not worry about people losing their telephonic communications!

The *Press* of 19 February revealed that Mr E. Croucher, verger at St Stephen's Church, had sustained an injury while felling a tree. He could not attend church, this being the first time in 60 years that he had missed Sunday duties.

A *Star* reporter had spent some time looking back at news 10 years ago from 1945. One reporter revealed that intruders had broken into the Martello Tower at Vazon and had taken away flooring, presumably for use as firewood.

Military officers at Fort George were offering a reward of one guinea for information leading to the conviction of the thieves.

Mrs Bertha Way, who eventually became the first woman undertaker in Guernsey, wrote from Biberach stating that her husband, James Way, was now deputy barrack leader and was very interested in that employment. Mrs Way was on a few weeks vacation from her duties – teaching in the camp school.

So the month of February came to a close. News at the front was good, despite what the front pages of the Guernsey papers conveyed. It would surely not be long before the Union Jack flew over the Channel Islands once more.

But, unknown to us, we still had March and April to face under German rule and with serious shortages and a low standard of living, what would these next few weeks bring?

Repaying the Red Cross

THE Bailiff, Sir Victor G. Carey, was very unhappy with the response from islanders to the Red Cross Fund that had been set up to repay the great help the organisation had given to Guernsey.

In a letter to the editor of the *Guernsey Evening Press* in March 1945, he wrote that he had been somewhat disturbed at the amount of the contributions to the fund, which had reached £17,220 and this after the fourth distribution of parcels. The value of the parcels was about £40,000 – this without taking into account the cost of transport from Lisbon.

'The civilian population, or at any rate the majority of them, are therefore living on charity which I am sure is repugnant to their feelings, and I cannot think that the smallness of the contributions to the fund as compared with the value of the parcels, is due to a large extent to the excitement which prevails at the time when an issue of parcels is made,' wrote the Bailiff.

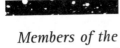

Members of the agricultural auxiliary police wore yellow armbands inscribed 'Hilfspolizei'

He concluded: 'I therefore take this opportunity of appealing to all, both rich and poor, who can do so, to contribute to this really worthy cause more liberally in the future, so that the amount which will eventually be handed over to the Red Cross Society may be more in consonance with the benefits which we have thankfully received.'

Children were now using roller skates to get to and from school. The *Press* reported that there had already been several minor accidents involving skaters. Some of the children seemed expert skaters others not so, jeopardising not only their own lives but others.

The German Commandant issue a notice banning the use of

■ FOOD FOR JERSEY: The Vega in St. Helier, Jersey

water for domestic purposes to drinking and cooking only. He noted that despite appeals to save water, island consumption had not been reduced.

The use of water tanks, flushing tanks in toilets was forbidden. Water closets had to be kept clean by using collected water. In future, the hours at which water could be drawn would be from 8.30am to 10.30am and from 6pm to 7pm. Water of a limited amount could be stored for preparing meals during the water curfew periods. The *Press* stated that contravention of this order would endanger the community and must be considered as sabotage.

It was thought essential by the occupying force to describe the uniforms being worn by German police who were entitled to search houses. First there was the Feldgendarmerie, who wore breastplates inscribed as such. Members of the agricultural auxiliary police wore yellow armbands inscribed 'Hilfspolizei'. Certificates would be displayed by detectives.

After being damaged by bombs dropped in the Old Harbour, the Town Church was re-opened for services in March 1945. The special service also marked Mothering Sunday. The sermon was preached by the Rev. William Kilshaw, priest-in-charge.

Readers of the *Press* were informed in March that the Vega would be making a further journey to the Channel Islands in April.

Existing stocks of flour would be so controlled as to last until the first week in April. A senior police officer warned would-be thieves of the danger of ransacking derelict houses. Floorboards in many instances had been already ripped up by illegal wood gatherers and this constituted a great danger to others who followed in their footsteps.

It was reported in the *Star* that a Mr A. J. Gillingham had invented his own type of match to fill the gap, which now existed in supplies of this product. He was now supplying 50,000 to 60,000 matches a week and was due to open a shop to sell on a retail basis. This gent was also hopeful of producing boot polish and ink.

Several issues after the Bailiff had complained about the slowness in which the Red Cross Fund was growing, the *Press* issued the improved total of £20,547.

A young girl, not yet four, uttered the following prayer of her own comprising: 'Thank you, Jesus, for sending the Vega with the parcels and the lovely, lovely white bread. Amen.' Her parents suggested that this prayer might be uttered also by older lips.

Gangsterism in Landes du Marche

DURING March 1945, a crime was reported at an address in Landes du Marche and it was described by the *Evening Press* as 'gangsterism of a type fortunately rare in the annals of the island.'

A farmer by the name of J. Mahy was overcome, bound up and robbed of precious stocks of food. Returning home after tending his cattle, the elderly farmer, on entering his house, was tripped and pounced upon by two masked intruders.

Although the houseowner grappled with the men, he was bound hand and foot with wire, which the thieves obtained from the household telephone. Cloth was placed over the farmer's face to prevent him calling for assistance. Potatoes, beans, rabbits and Red Cross parcels were items included in the haul.

The imported stock of men's shoes had now been exhausted. All that remained was a limited supply of second-hand footwear, which was also only obtainable by permit.

The German Military Court had in its possession a number of unclaimed watches believed to have been stolen. Islanders who had reported the loss of such watches could reclaim them at the German Military Court office in Mount Durand.

Children of the States Intermediate Schools were each given a quantity of cod liver oil and malt; this was a gift from the Red Cross.

It was announced in March that the Regal Cinema had reopened its doors for the showing of films. The Germans had allocated 50 seats at each performance for the civilian population.

A reader asked the editor of the *Guernsey Evening Press* why extracts from Red Cross messages no longer appeared in the newspaper. The editor explained that some messages sent through the Red Cross contained factiously conceived remarks, which had a political innuendo. Therefore, the German censor had ruled that such messages should no longer be published.

Peter Girard, who had been headmaster of the Castel School as well as the Intermediate School, was leaving the Castel. This meant that he could give all his attention to the Intermediate pupils. The *Press* paid tribute to his hard work for both schools during the Occupation. It was due, in no small measure, to him that children had enjoyed fires in their classrooms and those at the Castel School had been provided with midday meals from nearby soup kitchens.

Fishing was to be resumed and all catches were to be allocated on the basis of 60 per cent to the German forces and 40 per cent to the civilian population.

Petrol would be provided free by the Germans to owners of motorboats.

Catches would be processed at St Peter Port, St Sampson's and Portelet.

Deputy controllers were being recruited to ensure that fair play was seen to be done. This was obviously an attempt by the

■ PICTURE SHOW: The Regal cinema, a source of entertainment for both the Germans and civilians during the occupation.

■ HEALTH CENTRE: The Cartel Hospital was for all civilian emergencies during the Occupation.

Germans to help feed the troops who were now getting desperately short of food.

The authorities had decided not to issue a ration of Red Cross cigarettes to men only. This was because there were not enough smokes to include women in the issue. This was followed by letters to the editor complaining about the decision. One woman suggested that the men should have got their smokes, relying on them to give a gasper or two to their wives.

I think also the women folk thought a ration for men would make them less difficult to live with!

Going to hospital in March 1945 meant taking clean sheets and pillow slips with them and sending them home via relatives for washing.

Dog owners were reminded by the German Commandant that it was an offence to allow their pets to run free around the island. The animals might be shot and owners would face punishment.

A well-known firm was offering their tailor dummies for fuel.

The *Star* noted that the shopkeeper evidently anticipated a change in figures as well as styles, after the war!

With the food shortages so serious in the islands, the inhabitants were praying for a quick end to this Second World War. However, there would be the whole of April with which to contend and a few days into May.

Shortages persist as Liberation nears

AT THIS time the Channel Islands were moving into the last full month of German occupation. The enemy had flown into the islands in late June occupying Guernsey and Jersey first and then moving on to the remainder within days

Now, the inhabitants were really feeling the pinch but had been saved from a more serious plight by visits of the Red Cross ship Vega carrying vital food and other supplies.

On 4 April, the German Commandant revealed that two Georgian soldiers under his command were missing. These troops had come to Guernsey to increase the number of defenders, having thrown in their lot with the German nation. But they were not very enthusiastic.

I remember one Georgian soldier, who could speak English, providing me with up-to-date information as to the advance of Russian and Allied forces in the final bid to achieve victory.

Of the two Georgians missing, one was thought to have possibly suffered an accident. The second missing trooper had committed an offence and had deserted. The public were warned not to assist this man with food or shelter.

In the same edition, but not connected to the missing troops, the *Star* reported an attack on Mr J. de Garis, a farmer of the King's Mills. On investigating noises on the farm, he went to investigate and was set upon by one or more men. He sustained serious injuries. Another man who went to the farmer's assistance was slightly injured, but Mr de Garis found himself in hospital.

Hearing aids and X-ray plates had arrived from Lisbon to help islanders in their real hour of need.

The Germans were stepping up their patrols of country areas to try and prevent the theft of growing crops. Troops were told at night to shoot at any figures seen bending in fields to reap crops or entering glasshouses. It was becoming more than dangerous to venture out at night!

Local newspapers were to be published three times a week

instead of four to conserve supplies of newsprint and power. Both papers would be published on different days, the publication days being Monday, Wednesday and Saturday.

Invalids in Guernsey were to be examined with a view to being taken to a neutral country for treatment. It was anticipated that a hospital ship would arrive in Guernsey during the next six or eight weeks.

Of course, by then, the island would be liberated, but at that stage, nobody could visualise such an event.

The *Press* announced on 9 April 1945 that St John Ambulance was to open the mansion at Saumarez Park as a residence for the elderly. It would be a hostel run on modern lines and the warden would be Transport Sergeant John Dorey.

The Vega was due to arrive with more supplies, including seeds to replenish island stocks and boots and clothes for workers. The Bailiff appealed to people who were reasonably off with supplies to forego the next issue of Red Cross parcels so that people in desperate need might be fully catered for.

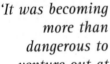

'It was becoming more than dangerous to venture out at night!'

Readers were warned to be on their guard against house callers who tried to strike bargains for valuables or food, and having left with the items, failed to return to complete the barter. Others

were calling on homes with tales of woe in a bid to play on good-natured people to the extent of their parting with precious foodstuffs.

Growers were informed that it was no use applying for seed beans as stocks were now exhausted. However, other seed such as table beet, carrots and cabbage had arrived via the Red Cross.

A farmer and his cowman, when milking their herd each morning, always partook of a glass of milk each as a refreshing start to the day. One morning they arrived in the stable for this purpose to discover that the cows had already been milked by intruders. However, as an act of kindness, the thieves had noticed the two upturned glasses on a shelf and had kindly filled them with the milk of kindness!

Donations to the Red Cross now totalled £28,066 following an appeal from the Bailiff to islanders to dig deeper into their pockets.

Ruette Braye couple battered to death

IN MID-APRIL 1945, the *Press* reported the violent death of Mr and Mrs George Robins.

They had been found battered to death at their home in the Ruette Braye. Food and money had been taken from the property. It was a great shock to islanders and it vividly

■ FEUDAL STATE OCCUPIED: German troops at Sark's Creux Harbour.

illustrated that there were now people in Guernsey ready to kill for food. An inquest decided that there was no doubt that the elderly couple had been murdered by some person unknown.

More than 100 people gathered at Le Foulon for the funeral of the couple. There were 47 floral tributes.

The Germans said in mid-April that they wanted 400 vergées of land for cultivation. They charged the States to supply to them details of all areas of 10 perch or over which were not to be cultivated by civilians that season.

This was obviously an emergency move by the Germans to try and maintain a supply of vegetables for their troops. But they would not need the food as liberation from their occupation of Guernsey was now just around the corner.

From the Potato Board came the news that the ration of spuds would now not last all that long. It had been hoped that there would be enough potatoes at least for a couple of months but due to pilfering, this was not at all certain.

From Sark came the news that islanders had raised £700 for Red Cross funds. This was £2 per person.

In Guernsey, it was reported that Jersey cows could now be seen grazing in local fields. Many Sarnians had received their first glimpse of these cows with their beautiful heads.

One letter writer noted that churches in Guernsey had united due to the circumstances. He suggested that the worship was much improved. This was surely better to have one place of worship filled than to have several churches languishing with small congregations and choirs.

A 15-year-old youth who stole Red Cross food from a house was given 12 strokes of the birch after appearing in the Police Court. He was considered too young to send to prison.

The editor of the *Press* wrote that it was unnecessary to publish several letters received on the subject of cigarettes as a decision had now been taken to divide the supply between the sexes and not confine rations only to males.

On 20 April 1945, Hitler was 56 and the *Star* carried this fact on the front page.

'The German people believe in his mission. The limits of the German sacrifices and the willingness to fight are the security of the victory of the Fuehrer and his people,' concluded this item of news.

Stamp supplies were almost exhausted and soon, said the Post Office, people would have to go to post offices and pay the cost of delivering in cash over the counters.

A young woman from the Vale had a shock when she was refuelling her fire with furze. A rifle cartridge was in the furze and it exploded and caused her to suffer an injury.

The clothing controller had a problem. Women were demanding that they wanted Red Cross stockings but there were only 600 pairs available and evidently there were 10,000 women demanding a pair each.

'How can it be managed?', asked Mr Lovell.

In a sermon at St James, the Rev T. Davis said that the organising powers possessed by people in Guernsey had not spread to the powers that be. There was more organising power in the humble women of God than in all the committees rolled into one. He accused the States of mismanagement of the food problem. Concerning the grave circumstances prevailing, I think he was being a bit unfair.

146

Hitler's death is announced

WHEN islanders glanced to the top left-hand corner of the *Guernsey Evening Press* on 2 May 1945 they read: 'The Fuehrer, Adolf Hitler, has fallen in the Capital of the Reich in the battle against Bolshevism. His successor is Gross-Admiral Doenitz.'

■ END OF A TYRANT: At last came the news that Hitler had died.

During the following days, tributes to Hitler were published. There was also an appeal printed from Reichsminister Speer to the German people to press ahead with the reconstruction of their country. He expressed his unshakeable belief in the future of the German nation.

For Guernsey people, the news of the death of Hitler brought relief. The end of the war in Europe must be near. Soon they would be under British rule again. Soon they would be getting vital supplies. Soon they would be re-united with those who had evacuated so long ago.

The main headline in the *Press* on 2 May read: 'Fanatical House-to-House Fighting Rages Day and Night in Berlin.'

In another front-page story, it was revealed that 1,000 English policemen were to be drafted to Germany to work in that country's occupied territories.

It was pleasing to read that the Guernsey Red Cross fund had now reached £35,221. This, evidently, included monies from Sark.

A member of the Anglican Church wrote to the *Press* on 2 May in reply to the remarks made by the Rev Davis of St James in his sermon. The vicar had complained about what he considered was the lack of organisation shown by civilian leaders in dealing with food supplies and suggested that the humble women of God could do better.

'I am of the opinion that the island community, including Rev Davis, owes a very great debt of gratitude to all the willing workers who made possible the distribution of Red Cross parcels; to the doctors who worked out the food values; and to the Red Cross committee,' wrote the Anglican.

He concluded: 'What is more to the point in thinking is that in addition to this, Rev Davis owes an apology to those workers whom his words labelled unclean.'

In his sermon, the preacher had also complained about Red Cross parcels being opened for some reason before delivery and perhaps affected by handling.

The use of mains water was now being restricted in use from 9.30am to 12.30pm daily. Before and after this three hour period, no water could be drawn for any purpose even if the pipes were filled. This order came from the Germans themselves and was also printed in their language for the benefit of the military.

There was no let-up in thieving across Guernsey. Livestock, bread, soap and books were being stolen. One man at St

Sampson's reported that he no longer had a shirt on his back. The only one he possessed had been stolen.

A Ulrich Schreier wrote a long article in the *Press* concerning the way, in his judgement, the Germans had supplied supplies for islanders during the war years.

He concluded with these lines: 'I have gained the impression that the German occupying authorities have fulfilled their obligation towards the Channel Islands and in accordance with the rules and demands of International Law.'

Islanders would be getting their eighth issue of Red Cross parcels on 9 May, which would coincide with the surrender of the islands by the German occupying power. There is no doubt that these shipments of food and other essential supplies saved the lives of some of the inhabitants. The food started to arrive at a time when stocks had dwindled. The Germans were suffering as much as the civilian population. It was suggested that domestic pets were being stolen to be killed and eaten.

A bag of Red Cross flour, which spilled from a train on its way to St George's Hall, was scooped up by a German soldier using his cap as a container. This I saw with my own eyes.

The Bailiff, Victor Carey, issued a notice on 7 May 1945, which stated that it had come to his notice that several people had recently been convicted of stealing or receiving stolen Red Cross supplies.

He warned that the Red Cross Supplies Committee had the power to withhold supplies from persons guilty of certain offences. This would be done in future.

Liberation!

AT LAST liberation from the German yoke had been achieved! Although it was 9 May 1945 that British troops once again stepped ashore at St Peter Port Harbour, the actual announcement was made the previous day.

The *Star*, under its editor Ken Gartell, published a one page edition on 8 May with the headlines: 'The War is Over for Guernsey – German Officers Inform Bailiff of Surrender'.

Islanders were told that they could listen to a speech by Prime Minister Winston Churchill at 3pm and immediately after that hour, flags could be flown as a sign of rejoicing.

On receiving this news, the Bailiff convened an extra special States meeting for midday where the full details of this momentous news was conveyed to members of the House. He also sent a member of his staff into St Peter Port informing tradesmen that they were free to fly national flags.

But, the Germans, who were to officially sign surrender terms, prolonged the issue. It was not until early on 9 May that this was achieved and British troops were free to land at St Peter Port and take military control of the island.

At 7.45am on 9 May, I had cycled from my home in Victoria Road to Glategny Esplanade to relieve the night shift of St John Ambulance personnel who stood guard over Red Cross flour stocks.

At about 8.15am came the news that English troops were moving up the north arm of the harbour. Rushing down to this point, I was thrilled to see the first troops ashore. At that time of the morning there were few people about, a fact that I have researched and remembered. But by 10am, the Town was teeming with islanders and at 10am, the Union Jack was hoisted outside the Royal Court building.

The Bailiff sent a message to King George VI informing him of liberation and begging him to accept the islanders humble duty and unshaken loyalty.

Brigadier Snow, Commander of the Armed Forces in the

150

Channel Islands, sent a letter to the Bailiff explaining that his troops would be working under pressure to get essential supplies flowing into Guernsey and Sark and asking people not to form crowds in areas where this operation was taking place.

The Brigadier also assured the Bailiff that German military would be moved from the island as quickly as possible.

It was promised that within two weeks Guernsey would be re-provisioned with all essentials. It was further revealed that

■ WELCOME CIGS: A British dispatch rider offers islanders cigarettes on Liberation Day.

preparations for liberation of the Channel Islands had been in progress for the past 12 months.

So the day passed, with more troops arriving in the afternoon of 9 May and even more on the Saturday. German troops had been ordered to assemble at a point inland, and really did not create any serious trouble.

Many would soon be leaving Guernsey for prison camps in the UK, but some would be kept back to carry out a spring-clean of homes and sites they had occupied and also to remove the huge number of mines they had placed in position mainly along low-lying coastal areas.

When the National newspaper arrived, islanders were buying as many as they could lay their hands on and branded medical items like Bile Beans were wiped up from chemists. It was such a novelty to see such items on sale and freely available again.

The *Guernsey Weekly Press* of 15 May carried pictures of the liberation activities and promised more when the necessary materials for processing could be obtained.

■ BACK-UP TROOPS: The days following the 9 May saw British troops arriving in Guernsey via the Old Harbour at the Woolworth's slip.

There was a report that minesweepers were now busily engaged in clearing the seas around Guernsey.

By chance, Liberation Day had also been Red Cross parcel day, and the *Press* commented that people knew that this time they could have a real tuck-in without the fear of depriving themselves of any future needs. For food and provisions would soon be coming through the ordinary channels.

In the midst of all the local activity and rejoicing, it was necessary to start planning for the return of the thousands of

Channel Islanders from Guernsey, Jersey and Alderney, who had evacuated, as well as the islanders who had been deported from Guernsey, Jersey and Sark to Germany.

They were freed by advancing Allied troops but Bill Damarell, of Rouge Val, St Peter Port, who was sent to Laufen Camp after serving his term of imprisonment in France for striking a German officer, escaped with a group of other people. They stole a lorry, drove through France and eventually arrived in Bolton. Bill was reunited with his wife and family. It was all very exciting!

Rebuilding begins

THE local newspapers of late May and throughout June carried important news as to how the Channel Islands were to be rehabilitated. There was much work ahead both for the British military and the local leaders.

At the earliest possible time, the Rev Jurat John Leale, president of the Controlling Committee, addressed a meeting of the States giving a review of the eventful years of the German Occupation.

It was a telling speech during which the president spoke of the difficult tussles his committee had experienced with the German military. Some of the German leaders, he suggested, had suffered from an inferiority complex and this had led them to assert themselves strongly.

'Our policy was based on a realistic acceptance of a situation which we all deplored, but which we were powerless to prevent. Our task was not an inspiring one: the most we could do was to make the best of a bad job,' he stated.

This was a very revealing speech and those who have been critical of the civilian leadership during those dark days would do well to read it carefully through. Perhaps their opinions would change!

Days in 1941 when large numbers of troops were being drafted into Guernsey were ones never to be forgotten. A thousand soldiers would enter the pier heads without warning and accommodation had to be found for them forthwith.

It was not unusual to have a demand from the military for 500 mattresses to be delivered at once.

There was an occasion when the Germans ordered the Controlling Committee to find 150 bicycles. When the desired number could not be delivered, the German Commandant decided that, for not telling him at once of the deficit, the Rev Leale was guilty of sabotage. He was ordered to find the extra machines forthwith. All would have been well if he had bothered to inform the Commandant earlier of the problem.

154

This, like other instances, showed the cat-and-mouse game being played and of the assertiveness of the German leaders.

The Rev Leale, who was to become Sir John, had tendered his resignation to the Bailiff, but it was not accepted. The British military made it clear that such an action at this time would be highly undesirable.

Newspapers were now reporting that 10,000 German troops had been cleared from Guernsey and 1,000 were being left to clear up their mess.

At present there was a cargo of oranges and 20 million cigarettes being loaded for the Channel Islands at Southampton.

Radio dealers informed the *Press* that they had worked hard during the Occupation repairing radios. The replacement of parts proved difficult, but in some instances when a German brought in a set for repair, the required part wanted by a civilian was removed and the soldier told that his radio was beyond repair.

The British troops were worried that live ammunition and firearms, particularly hand grenades left by the Germans, were now in the hands of young children. Parents were asked to question their children on this matter and discourage them from visiting German billets.

There was a tremendous amount of material abandoned about the island and I must say that on several occasions I wandered into German fortifications. One hut I entered was crammed full of German uniform clothing.

People who had taken part in entertainment were invited to the Central Hall to discuss future stage activity with an officer responsible for entertainment. Promoters of dances were also invited to attend. Things were getting back to normal.

The Regal Cinema was re-opening for civilians and there would be free performances. One to be screened was the story of the London Blitz. The North Cinema was also opening.

Some islanders had been seen wandering into areas where minefields were being cleared. This was said to be highly dangerous. It did not mean that the presence of troops in a field was an indication that the whole of the area had been cleared of explosives.

Guernsey was to have its first bumper Victory sports meeting on 20 June at the College Field. Members of the British Armed Forces had been permitted to take part in the festival.

The Bailiff received a letter from British Airways stating that the company was ready to resume air services to Guernsey.

A bright future beckons

AN EXCITING air adventure was recalled by the *Press* in June 1945.

Royal Air Force officer John Stedman had been saved from the sea by islanders nearly five years earlier and he wrote a letter of thanks on his return home from a prison camp.

It was in November 1940 when his aircraft had completed a photographic flight over enemy-occupied countryside and encountered a thunderstorm. The pilot made a forced landing in the sea. The crew of four took to a rubber dinghy and for two days they were tossed about on the high seas until land was sighted.

Towards evening on the second day, an 11-year-old schoolgirl at Portinfer, Vale reported a strangely-clad person on the foreshore.

A Mr H. Le Page, who lived nearby, hurried to the spot and saw an airman in full flying kit. Three more were scattered over the beach. Arriving also on the scene was a Mr T. Le Page, who noticed a fourth man in difficulties. He had been thrown out of the dinghy by the motion of the surf.

Mr T. Le Page entered the water and, assisted by Mr H. Le Page, managed to drag the airman to safety.

By this time, other islanders were arriving on the scene. The four airmen were taken to homes in the district and first-aid was rendered by the St John Ambulance Brigade.

German troops took the airmen into custody and there were threats to the Le Pages that they would be deported to Germany if the rubber dinghy, which had disappeared, could not be found. Later the dinghy was discovered washed ashore.

Thanks was also sent to Mr H. Le Page by the captain of the ill-fated plane. He explained that on that November night, he and his crew members were very dazed and were not sure who was helping them in their distress.

St John Ambulance Brigade had taken the airmen to the Emergency Hospital and Reg Blanchford recalled how he was instructed by the Germans never to do this again. Such members of the British armed forces had to be taken straight to the Victoria Hospital – the military unit.

A meeting of the Public Assistance Authority was called in June to discuss increasing the allowance for those receiving public assistance. It was agreed that for a single person, 5s increase weekly would be made, giving a total of £1. There were also suitable increases for families in order to enable the needy to purchase the new rations coming from England.

Fishermen were told to keep clear of dangerous areas in the Little Russel. Until further notice, no fishing or laying of pots could take place.

He spoke of a Nazi prison as 'a real hell'

The Sark correspondent for the *Press* stated that some inhabitants in that island were hoping that, since the Germans had been using motor vehicles, a move would be made to allow such transport in future, especially for the journey up the Harbour Hill. There had been no traffic accidents for five years and if their number of civilian vehicles were limited in number, it would prove a boon to all.

Of course it was not to be. Everybody had La Dame with which to contend! Of course tractors would be permitted and perhaps an invalid carriage or two but no further motorised transport.

People in Sark were moaning because war-time films from a British source were being screened in Guernsey but not in their island. Could not the authorities arrange some screenings in Sark? It was stated that the Germans had installed a talkie cinema in the Island Hall during their stay.

In Guernsey, the North Cinema was given permission to show films on Sundays, together with the Regal.

A Commission was to be established with a delegation in London for the purpose of ensuring supplies to Guernsey after the 90 days during which the military would be ensuring supplies.

Frank Falla, a former assistant editor for the *Guernsey Evening Press*, wrote home from his prison cell in Germany. He had been arrested and sent to jail for his part in operating an underground news sheet during the occupation. He spoke of a Nazi prison as 'a real hell'.

News was coming through of the earlier liberation of internment camps in Germany following the advance of Allied troops. There was bombing and shelling around such camps during the advance, but Channel Islands deportees survived to tell the tale. Everybody appeared to be getting to grips with the many problems that liberation had brought and the islands looked to have a bright future.